Out of the

Comfort Zone

The Church In Transition

by Dudley Hall

Distributed by:

MorningStar
PUBLICATIONS

P.O. Box 369 • Pineville, NC 28134

Table of Contents

Chapter One

The Transition Generation

I was shocked when I was told that in the early 80s George Gallup had opened an office in Princeton, New Jersey to monitor the next great awakening. I thought it strange that a man who was using the natural tools of polling and surveying could tell more about what was going on than those of us who supposedly had spiritual insight. If we could live 150 years from now, we probably would look back on these days with great appreciation for the work of God that is going on. We are *now* living in the midst of a tremendous work of God. It may be the beginning of the greatest transition since the early church.

I can remember the Jesus movement in the late sixties and early seventies. I can remember thinking with judgmentalism in my heart, "Those people are not really being converted. They are not doing it right." They were being baptized in swimming pools and in the ocean. They wore their hair long and unkempt. The people who were doing the baptizing were not all properly ordained. I later came to realize that my eyes had been so blind that I had missed being a part of a wonderful work of God.

Matthew 13:1-2 speaks about the householder who is able to reach into the treasure and take some things old and some things new. He says this man depicts the scribe who has become a disciple. *A scribe who has become a disciple is one who has made a transition from an old order into a new order.* He was given the responsibility of transcribing the scriptures into new text and was not only a good stenographer but an excellent theologian. It was necessary for him to be able to interpret the scriptures properly. A scribe was required to have a full commitment to the Jewish system, yet now this scribe has moved into the new order. He has heard Jesus' declaration that the kingdom of heaven is at hand. Having received this new revelation he has now moved from being a scribe in the old order to a disciple in the new order. This is truly a transitional man.

A wise householder is able to take the antiques of the past that are useful for the equipping of a modern house and bring them over. He is at the same time able to take modern conveniences and add them in with the useful furniture of the past and have a serviceable household. Have you been in a home that was totally decorated with antiques where nothing was allowed of the modern technology? Most of us would be uncomfortable operating with coal oil lamps and without running water, etc. That's refusal to move on with progress. On the other hand, to walk into a "pure" modern home where nothing of the past is allowed is to feel that you have walked into a sterile clinic. A wise householder takes antiques of the past and sprinkles them in with the modern conveniences of today. Now you have a house that makes you comfortable with your past; it creates memories of appreciation for days gone by and yet allows you to live in the technological advances of today.

God has had many transitions throughout history. He has raised up men, or generations of men, who have certain characteristics for leadership of the transition. Abraham was a transitional man. He was a man to whom God spoke unsuspectingly while he was doing his own thing in Ur of the Chaldees. Because of the personal revelation to him, he started an entirely new order of things and became the father of faith people. There was Moses, another man who encountered God. He was raised up by God to be a leader of a nation of people who could express His glory and show the rest of the people on the earth how society was supposed to live. There was Joshua who took them in after Moses had taken them out. As God began to inaugurate the ministry of the prophet, there was Samuel. Then came Elijah and Elisha, the prophets of power. King David transitioned from man's selection of kings to God's selection of kings. There are others, of course, but we come quickly to the transition between the Old Testament and New Testament. There is the transitional John the Baptist — the last representation of the old prophets and law as he announced "the kingdom of heaven is at hand."

Then, there is Jesus, the transitional person of all transitions. Before Him everything was partial and now everything was complete. The Scripture says that the law came through Moses but grace and truth came through Jesus. Then there was Philip who transitioned the giving of the gospel from Jews only to the Samaritans. There was Peter who took the gospel to the Gentiles. There was Paul who initiated the

whole missionary movement. Since Biblical times there were
men like Luther and Wesley. All of these men had some
common observable characteristics which lead us to believe
today, in this transitional generation, that there will be certain things we can look for to identify the transitional leaders
and those who will follow.

First, *each transitional man is internally motivated because he
has a personal revelation of God.* Without exception every man
who has been used by God to lead the transition has had this
personal encounter. He understands a revelation of a previous mystery. This encounter enabled him to be internally
motivated rather than externally controlled. Abraham had
an encounter with God and received life changing promises.
This required Abraham to believe. A passion was born in
him that caused him to move without any aid of external
evidence; he moved strictly because of the burning passion
in his bosom.

The same was true of Moses, who at times had no external
evidence to validate what God was saying to him, yet he was
unstoppable.

In the same way, Samuel was born a miracle. It is interesting how many of God's transitional people are born with
supernatural aid. Samuel's mother was barren; she prayed
and asked God for a son. God opened her womb and this
transitional man was born. Accompanying Moses was a
miracle of preservation after his birth. With John the Baptist,
Elizabeth had a barren womb, she also prayed and God
opened her womb. He too was born in answer to prayer.
With Jesus, not only was his mother's womb barren, but she
was a virgin as well.

In all of this God is speaking about that which He initiates. They start in the Spirit and operate in the supernatural. They are not limited to the natural principals of cause and effect. It is beyond logic, yet it is never illogical according to the mind of the Spirit. Too many have tried to be leaders in revival and awakening who are only operating according to natural principles and truths. Obviously it is not wrong to have children naturally, but God shows us His ways when He supersedes His natural principles to produce that which comes by faith and results in the miraculous. A personal revelation from God not only causes us to live life by faith, but it also makes manipulation unnecessary. The man who is internally motivated will not be manipulated by intimidation, domination, fear, guilt, peer pressure, etc. It is not these things that fire him up nor cool him down. His motivation is based on the boiling passion that moves in his soul; this is a result of the word of God that has come directly to him. It also makes it unnecessary for him to use manipulation in recruiting others to be a part of the movement. Since he himself is motivated internally, he is a minister of stimulation rather than a minister of manipulation. He speaks to the inner spirit of others who are born of the Spirit.

Another characteristic of the transitional man is that he will be misunderstood by the old order, thus he will be persecuted. All men tend to focus on the structure that life used rather than life itself. In the early days of the New Testament there was so much life flowing through the body of believers that they came to need some structure. People were meeting together, sharing with each other, giving their goods to each other as any had need. This was happening in such a flurry that there needed to be some administration. After prayer it was decided that deacons should be selected to channel the life that was flowing so abundantly. It seemed that the early church had this motto: "Make life beg for structure; never make the structure beg for life." They had so much life they needed structure to channel it and to keep it from getting out of hand. Since that day the church has kept the structure of deacons many times when there was no need for deacons. Many people today feel that a true church cannot exist without a board of deacons. Why have the structure if there is no life there? Much of what we see in our generation that has become identified with the work of God but is nothing more than the leftover structure that God used when life was there.

An interesting structure we have held onto which has probably outlived its real need is the use of certain building styles. Years ago in London a great preacher came forth named Charles H. Spurgeon. He was a mighty proclaimer of the word of God, and so much life grew up around his speaking that people came from hundreds of miles around to hear him. They constructed a building to house those who came and they called it Spurgeon's Tabernacle. It has been amazing to see how many miniature Spurgeon Tabernacles were built. The style was copied from that particular tabernacle. Perhaps people thought it was the structure that enabled the life of God to come. It was the truth of the word of God that brought the life, not the structure that channeled it. But men have a tendency to focus on the physical and the visible, associating the structure with memories of the life now gone. That is not a wise householder.

Several generations ago a man noticed the children walking the streets of a large city. Having a compassion born out of the life of God in his heart, he wanted to teach those children the truths of Scripture. What he started eventually became the Sunday School movement. It is interesting today how many people believe that you do not have an actual church unless you have Sunday School. We have held on to the structure and forgotten that it was the life that was the issue. Surely we aren't required to have Sunday School in order to have a recognized church in the kingdom.

Men have also held onto structure in the area of music. In every move of God the revelation of God is set to harmony and put to music. It is interesting how every generation will call their particular brand of music the true Christian music and everything that precedes it or follows tends to be scorned. The Scriptures give no particular style of music as Christian music. Again, we hold to the form and are oblivious to the essence of the life that was there. The life to be treasured is the communion of the Spirit and the revelation of truth expressed that comes forth through the music.

When God uses different men in different preaching styles we tend to pick up the language and preaching style instead of the passion that moves them. For example, we copy ministry models in praying for the sick, as if the technique is the key to success. Do they get well? Are the hungry fed? Do the blind see? Do the poor have the gospel preached to them? These are the signs of life.

I have visited some churches in recent years where it was believed to be something akin to blasphemy not to have the old fashioned altar call at the end of the service. If we did not sing a slow hymn and invite people to come to the front and take the pastor's hand and make "the decision," they felt like they really couldn't be saved. This is a terrible misconception. The issue is responding to God, not walking down an aisle or kneeling at an altar — not praying a particular way, or feeling a certain emotion or having a certain experience. The issue is responding to God.

Those who make the transition have the discernment to find the substance of life and are willing to be flexible with the structures of life. Any structure that is valued too highly will prevent us from making the transition. Jesus said the old wineskin will not hold the new wine. He did not say "maybe," "perhaps," or "sometimes." He said it will not happen. Those who get attached to old wineskins will be holding to the old wineskin while the new wine is being poured out somewhere else.

It is often said, "The greatest enemy to the new move of God are the leaders in the last move of God." What a tragedy, but it is a reality. Those holding tightly to the memories of the glories of the past days will be reluctant to yield to a new emphasis. "It was of God." "It was good." "God wouldn't do it another way!"

In the early seventies I was doing graduate work at Southwestern Theological Seminary. A fresh wind of revival was blowing in different parts of the land. I had heard reports but had not seen works of the supernatural manifestations of the corporate moving of the Holy Spirit. One day in our daily chapel service two young men visiting from Asbury Seminary in Wilmore, Kentucky gave a short testimony of a work of the spirit that had just occurred in their school. They told how people were spontaneously confessing sins, having reconciliations and making restitution. As soon as they shared, the same began to take place at our chapel. Men and women began to walk to the altar to weep and pray. Repentance from sins and confession was the order of the day. This went on for several weeks among the brethren. My own life was dramatically touched during this time. I found increased freedom from besetting sins and inner conflicts, while experiencing a new empowering. For months wherever I went the same phenomenon would occur on some level.

I now had a good experience, confirmed definition and expectation of what happens when the Spirit moves. I could now confidently say, "when real revival comes, confession of sins followed by freedom and power will be the model." I gave the testimony to many through the next few years. God honored my telling the story.

In 1982 I was part of a planned four-day conference on revival. On or about the third day, there was an unusual wave of God's presence. The spoken word was quick and incisive. People began to praise God openly and unashamedly. Some began to testify of physical healing, while others told about immediate deliverance from drugs and habits. Demons were being encountered and cast out by some who before didn't believe demons existed.

This was confusing to my perception of what was supposed to happen. There was little confession of sin. Could this be of God? Is it pure or counterfeit? My model almost trapped me. It was the same God with the same life but expressed differently. Many others didn't understand and persecution arose. It was not what we were expecting. It had not happened that way in 1970.

But God has ordained the persecution in order to purify His transitional remnant. Persecution has a way of delivering us from all external motivation and focusing us upon the revelation God is imparting. It is important that those who are following men be weeded out. Those who are hearing the call to march must be bonded only to Him and to the others who have heard if they are to express the purposes of God which produce life. We must not show a false sense of martyrdom, but we must recognize that if we go on with God those who are committed to the old order will persecute us. It is nothing new. That has always been the case.

The third characteristic of the transitional man is that each one will have a love for the people of his heritage; thus he will be humble. Humility is forever the key to walking with God in any generation. Paul the Apostle was a Jew whose training in Judaism had blinded him to the revelation of Jesus in his early life. He fought vehemently against Jesus and His followers. After his personal revelational encounter with Jesus it would have been very easy for Paul to have been bitterly opposed to Judaism and the Jews. However, when we listen to him pray, we hear him say, "I could wish myself accursed for my kinsmen according to the flesh." Paul was adamant about not allowing Judaism to infringe upon pure Christianity. On the other hand, he was committed to loving his kinsmen according to the flesh.

Even with Paul's great love for the Jews he would not allow even the Apostle Peter to bring compromise of the Jewish system into pure Christianity. When Peter compromised at Antioch with his friends from Jerusalem, Paul withstood him to his face. He writes in the book of Galatians that anyone who tries to mix any form of legalism with the gospel is accursed from heaven. There was no tolerance from Paul of bringing the old order into the new illegitimately and yet no bitterness is found in his life toward the people of his heritage; he was actually willing to lay down his life for them. The tendency today is for us to become arrogant and harsh toward the limited perspectives of our past. The fact is all of us got where we are, wherever that is, by some path made by the spiritual pioneers of the past, and we need to bless the path that God chose for us.

Stephen Mosely, in his book *The Tale of Three Virtues*, refers to humility as "light humility." I love that phrase because I see some people trying to be humble and it's awfully heavy. Stephen talks about a light humility that allows us to be real, to have fun and yet be humble at the same time. He says that the key to humility is admiration. It is a consciousness of being related to someone greater that you. Obviously, we are humbled in the presence of God for we see One who is the ultimate in greatness. But the point is that we can also be humbled in the presence of others when we see that God has used them to prepare and refine us and that in a sense they were greater than us.

I think about my own heritage growing up in a Baptist church in the South. Those who taught my Sunday School classes and led in my young men's group were not highly educated in Biblical knowledge. They would probably not be able to win in a theological debate. Yet they added things to my life that I could never have gained apart from them or someone like them. To these men and women who shared out of what they had, I give my thanks. I admire them for living up to the light they had.

Several years ago it was suggested that I was probably bitter towards my Baptist heritage, because of the limitation in my instruction about the supernatural and the gifts of the Spirit. I took that suggestion to heart and asked the Lord if it was true. I was trying to be honest about my own feelings regarding my heritage and the people of my past so I played a little game of word association. I wrote down the word Baptist and then what I associated with it. My first thought was, "Do I think of Baptist headquarters?" I quickly answered no. "What about Baptist Conventions?" Not really. "What about Baptist programs, emphasis on evangelism, commitment to the literal inspiration of Scripture and conservative interpretation of Scripture?" All of those I associated to some degree, but when I thought deeply I thought of Baptist *people.*

I thought about the people in Judson Baptist Association in southeast Alabama. It was a rural church, a white building with the tall sharp roof line. Outside were three red oak trees draped in spanish moss. On the porch was an electric light that dropped from the ceiling with a 6-inch chain for its switch. People who came there drove whatever means of transportation they had: pickups, cars and even a few John Deere tractors. When I was very young we only had a part-time pastor. He came to our church on the first and the third Sundays and went somewhere else on the second and fourth Sundays. We always had prayer meetings and if there wasn't a pastor to lead them, then one of the men in the community would. I was encouraged by both of my parents to attend the meetings and usually I did. It wasn't always out of the right motive and sometimes it wasn't very enjoyable, but I went. I went regularly to the Wednesday night prayer meeting not because I was so anxious to pray but because I thought it might help me, particularly if I had tests on Thursday. Maybe God would show favor toward me if I did something on Wednesday night that was religious.

When I was about thirteen, I was at one of these prayer meetings and something happened that today still helps to guide my life. We had gone through our regular program, sang three hymns (first and last verses) and one of the men had given a short devotional. He asked if anyone had any prayer request or word they wanted to share before we spent some time in prayer. A man had slipped in during the meeting who was a stranger. You could see several during the meeting asking questions like, "Who is that and who is he kin to?" When asked if anyone had a word he asked if he could share and he said something like this.

> For almost twenty years I have been a traveling sales-men and coming by this church on Wednesday evenings. Every time I would come by your lights were on. There were times when the weather was so bad that I was sure no one would be here. There were times when I would leave home and ice would be on the ground and the temperature would be near zero. I would bet myself that nobody would be at this little church. But your light would be on. Sometimes the cars would be as few as two or three and sometimes as many as fifteen or twenty, but someone was always here and your light was on. I have been a skeptic

all my life; in fact, I claim to be an atheist. A few weeks ago I finally came to the conclusion that my life was meaningless and that there had to be more than the shabby answers that I had found. In my search for truth I came to the realization that Jesus Christ was the answer to my life's needs. I gave my life to Him and I have become His disciple. I just wanted you people to know that in those years of my skepticism when I tried to argue against the validity of Jesus Christ, I couldn't get out of my mind a group of people who, regardless of the circumstances, always met together to worship. In my mind I could not erase the sight of a light that was always on.

As I think back about my heritage, I can honestly say that I will be happy if I never again have to be a part of services where we drag through the singing of a few hymns, out of tune and out of rhyme. It will please me if never again I have to listen to a sermon that is more information than impartation. I will be thrilled if guilt is not the primary motivation to challenge me to do better. I don't think I can stand going back to program orientation where our success is measured by how well we did the program, how many people attended, etc. But I stand in humble awe at the wonderful, sovereign plan of God. He has brought me to the point where I can honestly say that I have never met a Baptist yet that I didn't hope would come to know the fullness of Christ (for that matter, a Methodist, a Presbyterian or a Catholic). It is my desire that all of those who are walking in the light that they have may be given more light; that every person have the opportunity to walk in the true fullness of the everlasting life that Jesus came to bring. I find no pleasure in looking down my nose at my past or the people of my past. I am fully convinced they have added more to my life than I shall add to theirs. Because of their contribution there will be some in my generation to whom I can impart life. Even though Hannah was not a part of the prophetic movement her Samuel would begin, it was her travail that brought him forth to do it.

We are all living in wonderful days — days when God is again changing an emphasis and unraveling more of the mystery that has always been wrapped up in Jesus. We have an opportunity to be wise householders — to look into the past, strain out all that is unnecessary, purify the essence of the life and hold onto it. Reach into the new, take the good, remove the briars, cast away the excesses, and focus on the essence of life that God has given. We must carry the torch of the kingdom of God. These are not days for men pleasers or egotists. Men who are motivated by external motivation, afraid of persecution and haughty toward the past will not be men who hear the word of God and deliver it to this generation. The old wineskins are being recognized and discarded as the new wine finds its place in the new wineskins — men and women of humility and integrity who can endure transition.

Chapter Two
. . . .

The Church and the Kingdom

Only "Kingdom people" will stay in the flow of new wine.

Through the years of Christian history there has been much discussion and many divisions concerning the Kingdom of God. Whole systems of theological thought have been developed around certain views of the Kingdom. As is true with all doctrine, many well-meaning Christians have simply, and naively, adopted the view most prominent in their denomination. The result is their misunderstanding or confusion about one of the most important themes of the Bible.

It should not surprise us that there is controversy surrounding this subject; it is too important to be left uncontested by the enemy. When there is controversy concerning a subject, usually the church at large will try to avoid the subject altogether. But can we do this if we are to walk in the liberty of the Spirit of truth that sets men free? There will always be a spiritual fight over the "authority" and "power" issues. The truths of healing, deliverance, intercession, spiritual gifts and the kingdom will always be contested. It is through the proper understanding of these that victory is won and ground is taken by the body of Christ.

The concept of the kingdom of God was the basis for the great hope of Old Testament saints. They looked forward to that time when God's reign would be physically established on the earth. It would be a time of peace and prosperity for God's people as well as a time of blessing on all of His creatures. The political situation would be affected by the infusion of real justice into the corrupt political maneuvering of despotic governments. God's economics would bring God's blessings and cause the work of his people to blossom and prosper. They would lend to many but not borrow. The social conditions would be greatly improved as the poor would receive their supply and the needy would be helped. There would be righteous handling of the earth's wealth. The religious climate would be comfortably secure because God would reign on earth through His dwelling among His people and all people would look to Israel and His Jerusalem for their hope.

In the coming kingdom, people would be at peace, free from bondage, prosperous and healthy. This hope permeated and motivated the Israelites for many generations. It gave them comfort when they were slaves. It built courage when they were tempted to despair as the long years of captivity seemed to creep by. There was the ever-present, unending line of Amorites, Hittites, Jebusites, etc. that could make even the most optimistic saint wonder if victory would ever come. But there was always that promise of the kingdom that kept the ember of hope burning in their souls.

Because of their great hope, it was a monumental declaration that day when Jesus declared to the Jewish mentality, "You must change your way of thinking for the kingdom of God is at hand!" "At hand, what does He mean?" they thought. "If the kingdom is here now then what about the political, economic, social & religious changes that we've heard about? Why don't we see the changes?" The kingdom had come in a person — the King, spirit made flesh; and to see the spiritual kingdom they would have to be born of the Spirit.

Most of those who heard this declaration refused to believe, and they missed seeing what was already in their midst. They watched Jesus heal the sick, raise the dead, cleanse the leper, forgive sin, and rebuke demons, but never associated it with the kingdom. They had other explanations for these phenomena. Because they would not believe and could not see, they were sure this was not the long hoped-for kingdom, not only because it didn't resemble their expectations, but because they were sure they had not yet met the righteous conditions for the kingdom to come. After all, God would not bless sinners; and there were too many of them still around, even amongst the Israelites. So they missed the mercy of God while holding tightly to their perception of His holiness.

Sounds a little familiar doesn't it? Many still can't see His kingdom today because they don't believe we have qualified for blessing — "we aren't good enough." We've missed the essence of His kingdom. He justifies the *sinner*! He gives grace to the *undeserving* and the *needy*! It requires humility to receive the reality of the kingdom of God — the humility of a little child. Nothing humbles us like receiving what we know cannot be earned and would never be deserved.

Throughout Jesus' earthly ministry, the kingdom was His theme. He sent His disciples to preach and practice the kingdom. When He had finished his work on earth, he instructed them to teach others to do what He had taught them. Jesus was not content to preach the kingdom as a new theory, but a reality. Therefore He demonstrated it as well as declared it. He healed the sick demonstrating the superiority of His kingdom to that of Satan's. He cast out demons, obviously revealing His superior authority and power over them. He forgave sinners, raised the dead, and spoke to the raging sea. In every encounter with every earthly or demonic kingdom, He revealed superiority.

Some are quick to anxiously point out that He did not heal all the sick, raise all the dead, etc, and conclude that this proves the kingdom had not come. I think it would be more accurate to say the kingdom came but will not be consummated until the end of the age. There is the deposit here now, and the fulfillment will be realized when Jesus returns to the earth in bodily form. We receive some things now and will receive some things then. For instance, we have healing now and glorified bodies then; we have forgiveness of sins now and perfection then; we have victory over the enemy now and annihilation of the enemy then. So there is the reality of the kingdom *now* and the reality of the kingdom *then*. We must not delay the "now" aspects of the kingdom until "then," or try to force the "then" aspects to happen "now."

Those who postpone the kingdom totally are forced to live in an interim of exasperated unfulfillment and confused motivation. According to some who have this view, the kingdom is not going to come until Jesus gets back. He isn't coming back until things get so bad that the church will have to be snatched out in order to exist at all. If this is true, why should we be a part of preventing society from corruption and destruction? The faster things get worse, the sooner He'll return and get the original plan back into operation. The world is evil and corrupt and we are here to snatch as many souls into a temporary "foxhole" as we can. Don't get involved with filthy endeavors such as politics, economics, social issues, public education, etc. These are worldly and belong to the spiritually dead world. "Let the dead bury the dead," we hear quoted, "we must just win souls."

But win them to what? To be saved from eternal punishment is wonderful, but is that all there is to salvation? Are they to be left in their salvation "foxhole" simply to wait and warn everybody else to get into the "foxhole" with them? Sounds like a lower purpose for life than the eternal abundant life that Jesus talked about. Paul's "ruling and reigning in life" (Romans 5:17) sounds a little more exciting than the fearful refugee mentality of those who are "occupying foxholes" until the kingdom comes. What kind of hope and confidence can the church have when it is convinced that authority and power have been suspended? The church is not just a parenthesis in God's plan until He can get back to natural Israel. The church is called to be the light of the world and the salt of this earth, and it is difficult to be either with a foxhole mentality. Jesus did not leave healing in the hands of medical science, deliverance to the psychologist, and social change to the corrupt world system. He left all of them in the hands of His church!

To those who would object that saving the lost is our only objective, I object! Jesus said, "Going into all the world, make disciples; baptizing them...and teaching them to do what I have taught you." The key here is "do," not "know." What did He teach them to do, not just to know? To proclaim the kingdom of God and reveal its presence by healing the sick, casting out demons, cleansing the leper, etc. We are to save the lost, yes! But we are to save them to a life full of grace and glory now as well as hope for the fulfillment of the kingdom. They are saved to live in the reality of His invisible kingdom being made visible through people who live by its realities.

There has been some confusion because people have identified the church as the kingdom and the kingdom as the church. It is interesting to note that in the New Testament they are never equated. Jesus never taught us to preach the church. It was never intended to be the subject of our preaching or proclamation. Throughout the New Testament we are continually exhorted to proclaim and practice the realities of the kingdom. This is what the apostles did throughout the book of Acts, and it is to be included in the acts of the church until this age comes to a close. One of the last statements made concerning the ministry of Paul is in Acts 28:30-31, "And he stayed two full years in his own rented quarters welcoming all who came to him, *preaching the kingdom of God* and teaching concerning the Lord Jesus Christ with all openness unhindered." This too is what the church will be found doing until the end: preaching the kingdom and teaching about Jesus *with all openness!*

Some have argued that because the kingdom is not mentioned very much in the Epistles that it has been suspended until a later time. This supposedly validates the theory that the church is a parenthesis in the overall plan of God. A more accurate and appropriate interpretation would be that the church is seen as an agent of the kingdom. It is the visible expression of an invisible reality.

Focusing on the church as the message has only resulted in confusion and endless divisions. First of all, it produces disillusionment because the church is a living organism which will continue to flex and change her process toward maturity. She has not yet fully become what she is called to become. Therefore, the church will always be incomplete and imperfect until Jesus' return. When we preach the church, people are easily repelled because they see her many imperfections. The kingdom on the other hand is the rule of God. It can be confidently proclaimed in any culture and in any generation because the rule of God is never imperfect.

Secondly, those who proclaim the church as their central message end up with a mentality of self-preservation and competition. We want to protect our reason for existence as a local church. We become competitive toward all of those who are trying to get people to fill their churches. This translates into sectarianism and a provincialism preventing the unity of the body. It is the unity of the church that was the essence of Jesus' prayer for His people in John 17 and is the essence of its witness to the world. When our minds get so focused upon our own local assembly that we neither have time nor vision for the other churches, we have failed to discern the Lord's body properly. In the first century church

Paul declared this was the primary reason for the weakness, sickness and death in the church (I Corinthians 11:29-30).

It seems that every local church feels responsible to meet every need of the community. This is a subtle way of saying that no other church in the community is needed because "we will handle all the problems." This also promotes the belief that anyone who attends another church must be less spiritual or less committed than we are. The fact is that God has placed His many-faceted body over all the earth and not every local church is to meet every need of the community. Some churches will be called to focus on one area of need while others will focus on something totally different. When we begin to cooperate and love one another, the church really will become the "light of the world." Then we can provide the answer to the world's problems and darkness. It is only those who have a kingdom mentality who are able to relate on such a basis. Their allegiance is to the kingdom of God, not just to a local assembly. They are committed to God *through* their local assembly. This is not to become a "floating church shopper," but to have an overview of the purpose of God, a purpose which rises above our little parochial visions of the present. As the invisible kingdom of God is expressed through the visible agent of the church, the world begins to see that a higher form of living is possible. Anyone in the world can become a candidate for the grace of God.

KINGDOM STRUCTURE:
Who is the C.E.O. of the Church?

One of the significant failures of the visible church has been its adoption of the world's structure for its organization. In the absence of kingdom structure we have adopted the business world's corporate structure. We have pastors who act as C.E.O.s and deacons and elders who act as the Board of Directors. The rest of the people become the resources for money and ideas to carry out the goals of producing a good organization. Our success is too often measured by how many people we can get involved in our programs and in filling our buildings. The problem is that we can get a lot of people involved but they just don't go anywhere or really do anything.

Perhaps you have heard of the man who cut his right hand and was encouraged by his wife to go the hospital. As he entered the emergency room door, he was faced with two more doors. One said "Over 50" and the other "Under 50." Since he was over 50 he chose that door and walked through it. Again he was faced with two doors: "Upper Body" and "Lower Body." He determined that his injury was an upper body injury and so he entered that door. Again he was faced with two doors: "Internal" or "External." He determined that his injury was external and went through that door. Upon entering that door there were two more doors: "Major" and "Minor." He determined that the cut on his hand was minor and upon walking through that door found himself back on the parking lot. When he got home his wife asked him, "Were you helped at the hospital?" "No," he said, "But they sure are well organized."

We have often become skilled at getting people to go through the right doors but never really help them with their problems. In the kingdom, the focus is not just getting people to understand what doors to go through, but getting them healed, delivered and reigning in this life! Is there really any substance behind the doors we promote? When people enter through the living Christ they find life at its fullest.

In the kingdom we find Jesus, who is the King of the kingdom, being the actual Head of His body, the church. That means He is the One making the decisions and conveying them to those He has chosen to be the spiritual leaders of the church. The leaders He has chosen can be seen as the neck of the body. Their purpose is simply to convey the message of the Head down to the body. Then the body operates in unity and accomplishes the goals that the Head has set forth. If we are really connected to the Head we will get the same results that Jesus did with His ministry. The sick will be healed, the captives set free, and we will have access to God's provision for the present, yet our focus will turn from the temporary to the eternal kingdom. Such is the primary purpose of the manifestations of the kingdom which accompany the preaching of the kingdom.

When Jesus heard His disciples discussing who would be the greatest in the kingdom His answer to them was this, "In the world of the Gentiles you lord it over one another but in the kingdom of God it will not be so. He who is servant of all will be greatest of all." In that wonderful declaration Jesus gave the kingdom's principle of structure. It can be defined in two words — "mutual submission."

Mutual submission means that every person in the body of Christ gets to submit to every other person at some time or another. Since Jesus is the Head He gets to do the choosing and the directing. He picks by giving gifts to people and anointing them. Our responsibility is to simply recognize His gifts and anointings. How does Jesus appoint the leaders? By gifting them with leadership abilities. It is essential that a man who is called to be an elder or an overseer has the ability to oversee.

It is cruel to place someone in that responsibility who does not have that spiritual capacity. I remember when we started a church a few years ago. We had our eyes and ears open and were seeking to be attentive to God's choices for the leadership. One man whom we all anticipated becoming an elder was one of the most spiritual men in our group. He was physically and spiritually old enough to be mature in every way. He had a theological education for his background, his reputation was impeccable, and the thrill of his heart was to minister to people. Surely, we thought, he will make a great elder. As we began calling him into the meetings to help make decisions that required an overview of what God was doing, we found him to be frustrated and unable to function. It was at this point that God began to clarify for us the qualifications of leadership. It is not everyone who is spiritually mature that God has picked to be a leader. He doesn't just pick the well educated to be the teachers or the quiet ones to be the counselors. God gifts and anoints and we simply recognize His choice and submit to the one who has that gift. When someone is gifted with prophecy, we submit to that gift; when one is gifted in teaching, we submit to that gift; when one is gifted in the ability to oversee, we submit to that gift; when one is gifted to exhort, we submit to that gift. So we all end up submitting to others who have different gifts and callings. God designed the body to work like this so that interdependence would be necessary. Everybody has a place and must depend upon others in order for the body to be healthy. With this approach everyone has a sense of significance and importance. No one is seen as a second rate citizen and no one feels the unnecessary burden of having to be a leader alone. There is only One Head and that is Jesus. There is no competition for His part. All the rest of us are operating in our gifts, under our anointings, submitting to each other.

Man left alone to choose his leadership will always seem to choose one man. Just as the Israelites chose Saul to be their king, we will look for one man and place all of the responsibility upon his shoulders and create out of our expectations a role model for him that is impossible to fulfill. A modern day evangelical pastor has an impossible role model. If he succeeds with God, he will fail to meet the expectations of man; if he succeeds in fulfilling the expectations of man, he will almost certainly fail God in fulfilling His will. We often look to the Old Testament and Moses as our role model for the pastors when he was in fact meant to be a model of Jesus who is the Deliverer. When Jesus ascended He gave *gifts*, not *a* gift, back to His church.

Instead of giving one man He gave a multiplicity of gifts signifying that the leadership would be a team leadership and not an individual. This team, submitting to one another, and listening to the voice of Jesus, the Head, will be able to convey to the rest of the body the message that will keep the body healthy and in tune with the overall purpose of God.

In His infinite wisdom and ingenuity, God did not leave just one form of government to be the only form that the church could take. The only absolute rule is that Jesus is the Head and has absolute authority to make all of the decisions. God is infinitely diverse in His entire creation. He makes every snowflake different, He makes every person different, and He makes every congregation different. Regardless of whether a group of people choose democratic rule, eldership rule, or some other rule, mutual submission must be the order if kingdom structure is to be followed.

Chapter Three

The Church in Transition

How should we react when everything is shaking? The church is in transition. Jesus is preparing His Bride, and in this preparation there are great changes taking place. Any time there is change people will react to it; some react too much and some react too little. Our ability to deal with change properly will be a determining factor in how we are able to receive the Lord and what He is doing today.

Francis Anfuso says: "An ounce of reality is worth an ocean of speculation." Too often we do speculate about the church and about what God is doing and do not form conclusions from a solid Biblical basis. For example, consider a traditional church service: we have the call-to-worship, three hymns, an offering, special music, a sermon, an invitation, and we depart on schedule just like any other business meeting. Then we think that those who do not wish to attend our meetings do not care about the truth or are just plain carnal.

But this meeting is often based more on bondage to the familiar, speculation or simple sentimentality than on an encounter with God. We do many things for these reasons.

We sing certain songs because of sentimental memories associated with them. We hang on to certain traditions and rituals because that's the way they were doing it when we were saved or that's what happened when we were filled with the Spirit, or that's the way our mother or grandmother did it. We hang on to the past because it is comfortable.

No one likes discomfort. Many times we are kicked out of our nest of comfort — and our first inclination is to blame it on the Devil because "God always works in peace, and we're certainly not at peace now!" I can remember the first time I was in a church where people raised their hands and I thought, "Why do they have to do *that*?" And then they clapped. I didn't say it out loud, but inside I was begging, "Don't clap! You're putting Jesus in the same category with entertainers and superstars!" I was fighting against this change; it was uncomfortable for me. It had nothing to do with spirituality or Biblical truth, it was just uncomfortable. So discomfort becomes the enemy and we make the test of true spirituality whether or not we are comfortable. And to top it off, we misjudge our discomfort as discernment of the Spirit. We might as well say, "I knew it wasn't of God because I couldn't sleep during it."

That's one side of this issue: we fight change because of sentimentality, comfort, and tradition. But these old forms will not meet the needs of the people. We can accuse others of being unspiritual for not coming to our church, but the fact is we wouldn't show up either if it were not for religion. I have asked many preachers, "If you weren't getting paid, would you go to church every Sunday?" And in a candid moment, when I promised I wouldn't tell anybody their names, many of them said "no." Yet many in the church fuss at the world because they won't come to hear the church's outdated language, irrelevant programs, and uninteresting discussions.

There is another extreme to our problems. We have, at times, looked at the church with some objectivity and realized that people were not responding positively, but we allowed our culture to teach us how to reach them in place of the Holy Spirit teaching us. In many ways we've become just another institution with a market mentality. We looked at the businesses of the world with the shopping center mentality and we decided to try the same approach. Now it is not necessarily wrong to learn truth from sources outside of the church — the real truth will set you free regardless of where you learn it. But we have often been too quick to adopt whatever works for the world. As a result many churches have adopted a capitalistic, market mentality. And that philosophy is basically "the customer is always right." Now if the customer is always right, then you must give the customer what the customer wants, on terms that he will accept.

The December 17, 1990 edition of *Newsweek* contained a lead article entitled "And the Children Shall Lead Them: Young Americans Return to God." This article looked in depth at the growing trend of churches trying to please their "customers" (no longer called "believers"). This article discussed how commitment to a doctrine or truth was no longer considered important, that the "success" of a church was now determined by how good the programs were. It described how today's churchgoers inspect congregations like they do restaurants — if one does not fit their needs or tastes they just go to the next one. They no longer "convert", they shop for their churches! One pastor remarked: "The No. 1 rule of church growth is that a church will never get bigger than its parking lot." This new movement is called the Christian Growth Movement (CGM), which presents a businesslike marketing approach to church development.

I'm not trying to be critical of churches that are trying to grow, but what is the purpose of our growth? The article went on to quote one pastor as saying that the concept of individual sin is "kind of lost," because "people want support, not salvation, help rather than holiness."

There can be something very **right** about wanting to meet the needs of people instead of sitting back in our comfortable forms and playing church. But there is something terribly wrong with letting the people dictate the terms of their salvation. Jesus did not do it; the apostles did not do it and neither has any true leader of the Biblical or historic church. There is a religious inclination in man that causes him to seek water to quench his spiritual thirst, and to find bread to feed his life-starved soul. However, man will inevitably try to buy what he defines as his needs on his own terms, as cheaply as possible.

Marketplace success is declared when the product is quickly consumed by the masses. So how do we know when a church is successful? When "consumers" buy the product? When the buildings are full and people attend the programs, a church is considered "successful." We may read about some of these extreme forms of distorted priorities, but to what degree has the marketplace mentality affected us all?

A discerning historian once wrote concerning the gospel: "What began as a movement in Jerusalem became a philosophy in Greece, an institution in Rome, a culture in Europe and an enterprise in America." But is that what the gospel is meant to be? Is there an alternative to this mentality? YES! And I believe we see that alternative in the one whose life was devoted to foretelling the coming of this gospel — John the Baptist.

John the Baptist is one of the greatest illustrations of a transitional man. His ministry is a transitional ministry: a transition from the Old Testament of law to the New Testament of Jesus and the fullness of mercy and truth. John represents the Old but he embraces the New, so his ministry can be a pattern. There is so much that we can learn from him about how God operates when times are changing.

God does not yield to the mega-church or to the market, capitalistic mentality. He did not poll all the people of Israel to ask them what they needed. In fact, if He *had* asked them they would have said that they needed a strong military leader to free them from Rome. What they were sent was a Lamb who could free them from Rome and every other yoke. But Jesus starts freeing us from the inside out; they wanted to be freed from the outside in.

It seems strange to us that the Lord did not debut His great preacher in a metropolis — He sent John the Baptist, the first one to bring the direct word of God for over 400 years, to start his ministry in the Jordan wilderness of all places. Today we would call that a "bad location."

John did not have very good style either. Camel hair clothes and a shabby leather girdle were not the height of fashion even then. Nobody told John that you're supposed to wear dark suits and red ties and dress for power. Neither did his diet of locust and wild honey meet with much approval. John was a perfect example of bad public relations and poor growth strategy. The only thing John had going for him was the anointing!

Is God just ignorant of how to grow a church? John's message was the coming of a new order. New orders do not follow trends; they set them. John's beginning in the Jordan was one of God's ways of sifting out those who just wanted to be in on the *movement* from those who were *moved* by the message. The people had to go out to John; John didn't come in to them. If you have the anointing and the message for the times, you will not have to promote yourself.

It's interesting to note how many little "John the Baptist" ministries God is starting out there. Small rural towns are now becoming beachheads for the works of God. The *Fort Worth Star-Telegram* recently carried a story on one of these ministries located in Peaster, Texas. Peaster is a **small** town. They have a Post Office and a school, but the last time I was there, they didn't even have a store. You could stand on the church steps, toss a pebble, and hit the roof of most any house in town. Against the tide of popular CGM mentality, John Anderson went to Peaster to preach.

John had been divorced in his early life and had been disqualified from ministry in some men's eyes. But he still felt the call of God in his life and was thrilled with the opportunity to minister in Peaster. He didn't feel banned from God or relegated to the wilderness; he was just glad to have a place to preach. John started with seven souls at the Peaster Church and just preached the gospel and loved the people. Today their building seats almost a thousand people and there is a divine witness in rural Texas.

I'm not saying it's wrong to have a church inside the city limits, or in population centers; God is certainly moving to touch the cities in this day. I'm just saying that we should not operate on the capitalistic market mentality of giving the people whatever it is they will buy. John the Baptist preached a message of life. It was a hard message, but it had life-giving power. It was a message of a new order. The transitional messages will have that quality that sifts out the pretenders while imparting the hope that change is coming. John was saying that things were not like they used to be; he proclaimed a new kingdom that required a change of mind and change of values. Changing their minds would ultimately change their lives. He emphasized that you do not add the kingdom of God to anything else. "When you get into this movement," he was saying, "you're going to trade all your jewels for one 'pearl of great value.'"

There was a key to John the Baptist's message that is the key to every transitional message — the Bible says that "the word of God came to John." A lot of people try to preach a hard message like John the Baptist but nobody comes to them. Not only is it inappropriate to let the people tell you what they think they need, it is also inappropriate for the messenger to assume he knows what the people need — the message must originate with God.

Much of today's prophesying and preaching is man's opinion of what's wrong, and it focuses on sin and on changing the externals. But when John came he started talking about a kingdom that changes the internals. It was an internal message of external life. Multitudes started flocking to him — even in the middle of the wilderness. The religious leaders came, the poor came, the sinners and tax-gatherers came, the soldiers came: every sect of society came. And what does John say? According to the highest standards of good Public Relations he declared — "You bunch of Snakes! What are you doing out here? Who told you to flee the wrath to come?"

In essence, John was saying that you cannot just add the gospel to your little collection of gods. He preached repentance — the people had to change their minds and exhibit that change. And the multitudes begged him to tell them how they could apply this message to their individual lives. You must preach life in order to get people to respond to you like that. And John gave them specific examples. Every man who has two tunics must share with him who has none. If you have food, give to him who has none. John was saying that knowing the truth will make *people* the issue instead of *things*.

Tax-gatherers asked, "What does it mean to us?" John said, "Here's what it means to you. Be honest." Isn't it wonderful that God's life is so direct and so simple? John the Baptist didn't have to write them out a fifteen page sermon or a book on ethics to tell them what it meant.

The soldiers came next. And John told them not to take money by force, not to accuse anyone falsely, and to be content with their wages. In other words, don't abuse your position.

Notice what John did not say. He didn't say that commerce was wrong. He didn't promote capitalism or socialism. He did not even speak out against militarism. He talked about internals. This is the directness of God, the simplicity of God, the life of God.

John came into all the districts around Jordan preaching a baptism of repentance for the forgiveness of sin. That was the key to his message, and that is what God thinks the masses need. Instead of polling the people to hear what they "need" — a place to get together and have their own little club, a Christian community where everything is under one roof, a support group for various deficiencies and affirmation for self — God said that He knows what we need: we all need to be forgiven. When you are really forgiven you are freed from the guilt and condemnation that has crippled you and you are liberated so that you can forgive others. Then we won't have to get together for the affirmation of others, we will want to get together because we love each other and want to serve one another. The only thing that really keeps us in bondage is either not receiving forgiveness or not giving it. That is, quite simply, what John came preaching.

Notice John's attitude in all of this. He said, "Jesus must increase and I must decrease." Unfortunately, when things are going well and you have a message of life to which people respond positively, the tendency is to become an end unto yourself. The transitional church, if it becomes an end in itself, will become a part of that which is passed by. *Now*, more than any other time in history, we are called to decrease as Jesus increases. In the days to come you are going to see the temptation to be drawn to what the church is doing: the prophecy, the healings, the miracles. We are going to walk into a day when not just two or three in an assembly can prophesy but **all** can prophesy. His Spirit is poured out on **all** the sons and the daughters. Miracles are going to happen and the tendency is going to be "Look at us!" This must not happen. We must decrease; He must increase.

We must also be willing to be nonessential. John the Baptist finally had his head cut off. His ministry was not a long-lived ministry — it was a *transitional* ministry. He was persecuted because he stood for the truth in a world of deceit. His message contradicted the mentality of the day. John kept magnifying Jesus instead of making a name for himself. Individually or as a church we may not have our heads cut off, but we must be willing to be dispensable. If we are not willing to live with a dispensable mentality, when the greater ministry comes, we will end up competing with it, and ultimately persecuting it.

If God says one morning, "O.K., thanks guys, you did a good job but now your job is over," we must have as much fun closing the ministry down as we did building it. Otherwise we will become self-preservationists with territorial rights which are controlled by territorial spirits.

Consider the life of Jesus. In Luke 4, Jesus is baptized, goes out into the wilderness, is tempted by the Devil, and then comes back from his temptation. Verse 14 (KJV) says, "Jesus returned to Galilee in the power of the Spirit and the **fame** of Him spread throughout the surrounding districts." The Greek word translated "fame" is "pheme." It can be translated "rumor." The rumor about Him spread throughout all the surrounding districts. Do you know that when God starts doing new things in your church, or in your own life, rumors start? People will always speculate.

The second occurrence is found verse 37. The King James version uses the word "fame" again. It says, "and the **fame** of Him was getting out into every locality and surrounding district." This is after Jesus had begun to heal and cast out demons. The word for "fame" has changed here; it is the Greek word "echoes." This same word is used in other places to talk about the "roar" of the wind and sea. What used to be a rumor is now a roar. It will get rough as you go through the transition. There will come a time when the rumors become so loud you can hardly hear what God is saying, and sometimes you don't. Even your friends may turn against you.

The third time this word "fame" is used in relation to the Lord's ministry is in Luke 5:15, "The **fame** of Him was spreading even further and great multitudes were gathering to hear Him and to be healed of their sicknesses." This Greek word translated "fame" is neither "pheme" nor "echos", but "Logos" — the word of God. The truth finally gets out. But why must we go through the first two stages? It purifies us; it gets the false motives out and determines if we are truly going to respond to God or if we just wanted to be doing what everyone else was doing. If we are to make the transition into the new move of God we will be tested on this point — the rumor and the roar will get so loud that if you *can* be talked out of it you *will* be talked out of it. But if you will keep going there will come a time when the "logos" will prevail. Scripture says that the people began to come from everywhere because they wanted to get healed of their sicknesses. They saw life and they wanted it.

Of course, there are hazards even here. People love life, but they are not always ready to receive it. When life begins to flow people are drawn to it, until that life starts to contradict their tradition. At that point, they realize that if they go any further they must deny their traditions and receive criticism. At that point many return to the old ways.

Since we've been called to walk through transition let's consider these observations. The institutional church is locked into many traditions. This is not meant to be a negative statement; it is merely a fact. God can overcome our traditions, but it takes nothing less than God to do it. On the other hand, the market mentality operates on the premise that it is to provide for all the needs of the community — with the implication that other churches really are not needed (and are probably getting in their way.) The mega-church mentality tries to eliminate the need for any other church to be in town. Such a mentality says that God has not individually gifted the rest of the members of the body nor the other families that are in their territory. God gives every legitimate congregation a personality and an assignment, just as He gives every member of the body. So when one church has a program that is working and being blessed we do not need to copy it. We are not shopping centers in competition with one another. We need to bless other churches, support them, help them, and work with them, not against them. Any part of the body that only consumes for itself without regard for the rest of the body is a cancer.

One of the crying needs in the marketplace is that men tend to believe that a name will give them an identity. When a child is born out of wedlock, people say, "Give him a name," but what that child really needs is an identity, not a name. He needs a relationship. There are people in the church today who feel disenfranchised because they are no longer Baptist nor Episcopalian nor Charismatic nor Pentecostal — they do not know what they are. Some of these are beginning to cry out "Give me a name." People come to the church I attend, wanting to take on our name. We must say "No. That is not what we offer you. We do not offer you a name, but we will offer you a friendship. Would you like to submit to us and have us submit to you? We will offer you a relationship — but not a name."

If you have the market mentality and you poll the people, they will tell you that they need a name! They want doctrines and standards that define them and differentiate them from others. They may not use the word "denomination" but when you give them a name only, this tends to separate them from others who do not have that name. And when an outsider asks why we have one name instead of another, we magnify our differences in order to give ourselves a reason to exist. That is how denominations get started. They came out of a desire to be secure, to have an identity. But let me tell you — you have an identity. You are a child of God; you are related by blood to the rest of the children of God.

Is that too idealistic? Do we have to start more denominations? Are our grandchildren going to have to destroy again what we are trying to get out of right now? God is offering us an alternative in this transitional time to say that it will work if we will get a word from God like John the Baptist. If we will preach life, simply and directly — if we will give people a relationship and forgiveness, then it will work.

We are living in some of the most wonderful times in history. In the years ahead it will be said that these days were days of the greatest awakening in the church since the reformation — and perhaps since the birth of the church. Let us, like John the Baptist, keep our eyes on Jesus; let Him increase and let us decrease.

Chapter Four

I Will Build
My Church

These words have been a great encouragement to me. I admit that I have sometimes worried about the success of the Church. I wonder how something so focused on organization, yet so disorganized, can long sustain the apathy of the casual Christian whom the Church depends upon for survival. As a young boy, I wondered why people would leave such warm, comfortable homes to go to church where they would look and feel miserable listening to poor oratory and even poorer music.

When I was called to the ministry, I was not too excited about spending my life perpetuating this boring social institution. My call was from God to follow Him. Had it not been for the excitement of knowing Him, I would have had much trouble making a commitment to "full-time ministry."

God has taken me on a wonderful journey of knowing Him and learning His ways. I have come to understand that the Church is His people, the Body of Christ. I love the church but I just have not always understood what it was really supposed to be. The only models I have seen came from the corporate world where the emphasis was on the organization, where goals for success were set and measured. One can rise or fall in the ranks of leadership based largely upon who they know. The good churches have good presidents (pastors) with a good supportive board (deacons) behind them. One of the most important aspects of success depends on good hired help (staff). If all of these are in place, the clientele (congregation) responds favorably by committing their time and giving their money to keep the necessary programs going to reach the set goals:

1. A certain number of people attending;

2. A certain amount of money given;

3. Space limited to provide for the number attending.

Somehow, this doesn't seem to fit the New Testament model given in the book of Acts and amplified in the Epistles. There, the common characteristic was life. Those who believed in Jesus were part of the very life of God. It was the most exciting, most important reality they had ever encountered. There was no casual Christianity for several years after the Church was established.

The Church was not a place, nor a program, nor an organization — it was a living organism which had divine life. The more it was opposed, the more lively it became. It was not an optional activity for the Christian to consider; it was life. To reject it was to reject life and embrace death.

It is this living Church that Jesus builds. You are aware of the occasion on which Jesus made a well-known statement about the Church. Peter had just confessed that Jesus was the Christ, the Son of the Living God. Jesus used a play on words as He said, "You are Peter (rock), and on this rock I will build my Church." Many a theological discussion has been had concerning what Jesus meant by this statement. Was it Peter who was the foundation of the Church? Or was it his confession? Or was it all of the above? In a sense, Peter was a foundation stone. It was Peter who was used by the Holy Spirit to open the Kingdom to the multitude of Jewish people at Pentecost. It was Peter who was used by the Holy Spirit to open the Kingdom to the Gentiles of the house of Cornelius.

Jesus does not seem to mind building his Church with men. Imperfect, immature and limited men have always been His building blocks. It is part of His mystery and mystique. He is not building a theological system. He is building a Church using men who are not static, but always changing and being changed by Him.

But Peter, the man, cannot be explained apart from his confession. The content of his confession is the very heart of the Church. Jesus is God's appointed, anointed One. No other man stands on the same ground. He alone is the Lord, the head, the decision maker. All else is incidental to this great truth. Deny this, and you deny life. Confess this out of a believing heart, and you reign forever with Him.

However, not only is the content of this confession foundational, the act of confession is just as important. Divine life is not just a silent, private experience with God. The writer of Hebrews calls the Christian life "our confession." It is inevitable that we confess what we believe. It is that confession which not only seals the confessor for life but plants seeds which take root in the hearts of those who hear. The

Church is built on the shared testimony of those who have encountered true Church life themselves.

But the uniqueness of this confession of Peter was that it was not a product of his own deduction or mental awareness. The beginnings of the confession which made a man God could use into a foundation stone was a revelation from God to Peter. Jesus is not building a Church on man's abilities to discover truth but on the revelation that He Himself gives to men who have ears to hear. Jesus is building His Church of men who hear God and then live on the basis of what they hear.

Another astounding reality that truly encourages any lover of the Church is this: *Jesus assumed total responsibility for completing the building project.* **"I will build My Church."** Finally, we can relax! Even though He will use us in the work, it is not our strength or ability that will get it done — it is His job!

Recently when God whispered these words again to me, "I will build my Church," I heard another powerful implication. It was as if He were saying, "I'm not building ministries, organizations, institutions, evangelistic associations, mission programs, etc. My whole priority is to build My Church. If you want to be where I am, I'm building My Church."

That the Church is a priority in Jesus' heart is revealed in Ephesians 2:19-3:21. The mystery that was hidden from the Old Testament saints but revealed to the New Testament believers related to the Church. The Church was in God's heart from the beginning. It was not an afterthought. It was not "plan B" that God resorted to when "plan A" failed.

Those who are enamored with the uniqueness of Israel must know that God's promise was first and always made with Abraham and his seed (Galatians 3:15-18). God's people have always been those who believe as Abraham believed. Jesus is the seed of Abraham, and those who are "in Him" are the people of God.

God's priority is not a physical temple (Ephesians 2:20-22) in Jerusalem, nor a physical nation by any name, but a Church through whom He can show His mercy and power. God's people are those who, by grace through faith, have received Jesus as their Lord and Savior.

It is through these people that God chooses to infect the world with righteousness. Governments are important, but on God's priority list they are under the Church. Technology is important. So is education, disarmament, ecology, and equality in the marketplace, but these are only minor issues compared to God's Church. Do you comprehend this? The Church is God's life on earth. Everything else on the earth pales in comparison to its glory and significance.

Believer, if you grieve because you feel the glory days of the Church are in the past, take courage. Jesus is still building His Church. It is a process, and He is not finished yet. When He undertakes a job, He finishes it to total perfection.

Some want to despair over all the division and controversy today. Do not despair. Rejoice! The old structures will fall as life breaks forth into bigger expressions. Structures built to handle the revelation of the last generation are not big enough nor strong enough to handle what God is saying today.

Remember, His Church is His life in people. The Church is alive! It has in it all that is necessary for life and only needs nurturing. The Church has a Head and many body members which will function if given a chance.

Do you remember how disappointed the Western Church was when Communists took over China several decades ago? There had been a great outpouring of the Holy Spirit just before the takeover. I remember the laments of the missionaries who said: "The Church will die. The Communists ran off all the leadership. There is no one to direct the people, nobody to organize, no one to correct their theology." A few years ago when we could find reliable sources to give an account of the Church in China, we learned that it may be the healthiest Church in history, with numbers ranging from millions to hundreds of millions of vibrant, loving, living believers who have discovered that the Church is an organism with God's life in it.

One of the hardest realities for the Western Church to face is the practicality of the headship of Jesus. We are so accustomed to having a visible head of our institutions and organizations that we find it difficult to believe Jesus will direct His Church on a daily basis. We seem to forget it was through a revelation heard by a man who believed it and confessed it that we received Jesus' promise to build His Church. We tend to be much like Israel who rejected God as their invisible king because they wanted a visible king like other nations (See I Samuel 8).

Do these motives sound all too familiar?

> *"We want someone visible to judge us, to tell us what is right or wrong. We cannot hear God for ourselves. Give us someone to interpret God's will for us."*

> *"We want someone visible to glory in. All the nations glory in their strong, gifted leader. We want to brag on our leader (pastor?)."*

> *"We want someone to fight our battles for us. We will pray and pay for someone to fight the devil while we do our own thing."*

God gave Israel what they wanted and told them what would result: they would be used by the visible king for his goals and purposes until they cried for relief. This sounds a lot like the Church in America, doesn't it? We reject the headship of Jesus and ask for leaders who invariably lose favor in our eyes. And then we look for another.

Jesus gave the Church apostles, prophets, evangelists, pastors and teachers to equip the body members to do the works of Jesus. To a great degree, we have rejected the role of apostle and prophet and redefined the role of evangelist to fit our needs for numerical success. We have made the pastor/teacher the visible king and required him to do that which is impossible. If he succeeds with God, he will fail with man, and vice versa.

To receive Jesus' headship is to receive His gifts to the Church, and then to hear Him through them. We are all priests with the privilege of hearing God for ourselves, but God has set some in the Church to give corporate directions. These must be recognized, received, and released.

We don't have all the particulars worked out, but that is part of the wonderful journey of knowing Jesus. God is speaking as certainly today as when He spoke to Peter. We must hear His "today" word for the Church. It is but another plateau of Jesus building His Body.

The body life the early Church experienced (Acts 2:42) was but a foretaste of what we are to experience as we learn to share the life of God in Church life. We are not there yet, but do not despair. Let's live His life, and Jesus will finish His project. Don't settle for anything less than *His* Church!

Chapter Five

Truth Versus Error

One of the greatest enemies of the people of God is fear. One of the great promises of God is found in II Timothy 1:7, "For God hath not given us the spirit of fear; but of power, and of love, and of a sound mind."

The first part of this verse tells us a lot. First, it tells us that fear is a spirit. It also tells us that fear does not come from God, so obviously it is an evil spirit. It's no fun being ministered to by an unholy spirit.

There is no in-between spirit. We are either being controlled or ministered to by the spirit of power, love and a sound mind or we are being ministered to by a spirit of fear.

Fear can be an unconscious thing. Sometimes even the fear of fear will set the course and direction of our life as we do almost anything to avoid a confrontation with it. We must ask ourselves, what is really controlling our life? Is it love, power and faith? Or is it fear, worry and unsound thinking? We do not have to fear anything or anyone on this earth but God. If we would fear Him properly we would not have any destructive fears in our life.

In II Kings chapter 17 God allows His own people to be dominated and plundered by a foreign power which is controlled by Satan. Please consider that this is what has happened to many of us — we have been given by God into the hand of the plunderer, and the plunderer we are talking about is the spirit of fear. God does this for a reason. He responds to the rebellion of His people *in order to drive them back to Him.* When fears begin to dominate our life, we need to examine ourselves. Have we departed from the Lord and His purpose for our life? When we are abiding in Him and are submitting to His will in the pure and holy fear of the Lord, there is no room for other fears in our life.

In verse 23 we read that "Israel was carried away into exile from their land into Syria until this day." Israel was put under bondage and they began to worship the false gods. As we read on in this narrative we see that God then responded to this by allowing some of the people to be destroyed by lions. The king of Assyria decided that some of the old priests should be brought down to teach the people how to respond to their God so He would be appeased and not send out any more lions. He sent a priest down to teach them how to fear God.

This was a terrible mistake. This is the conclusion of an unsound mind working in the king of Assyria. He was thinking, "Let's just satisfy all of the gods; let's satisfy this God and our gods and let's bring priests in and teach this group how to fear their God so we can appease all the gods." But that is one thing you cannot do with our God — you cannot mix Him with others. He refuses to mix. So they erred in trying to teach the children of God how to fear God *without removing all other gods.*

Basically, that is often what we have done in conservative, evangelical Christianity with our emphasis on Bible teaching and Bible study. We have tried to teach people to follow the precepts of God without requiring them to remove all foreign gods. We insist, "I am a Bible believing Christian." But we also have many other kinds of little gods in our lives. When we still have other gods, we will also have other fears. Idols in the Old Testament were not just what the people worshipped. They were what the people feared. What we fear is what will control us; therefore, we should only have one fear in our life — the fear of the One God.

Beginning in II Kings 17:29, Scripture tells us of the many different gods worshipped by the people of Israel in their captivity. God reminds them to be faithful to Him in verse 37 when He declares: "You shall not fear other gods." Then He states in verse 39, "but the Lord your God shall you fear, and He will deliver you from the hand of all your enemies."

We only fear a god. If we have another god, we will fear him. So what does that reveal about our fears? It means for every fear we have, we have at least one god. And God has said He only wants you to fear one person. How simple and free our life would be if we only feared one person, if we only cared what one person thought, if we only had to please one person! There is no greater liberty or peace that we will ever know than when our life has been restored to the simplicity of fearing only one God! It is not enough to fear the Lord *yet* have other fears (gods); we must fear Him *alone*.

What are some of the other gods that we fear in this day? Some people fear failure. If you fear failure, who is your god? Success. Do you realize how many people are motivated by the fear of failure? They do what they do because they don't want to fail. Some men work themselves into exhaustion by taking on two or three jobs. Why? They want to be successful. They do not want to be considered a failure.

Many of us try to live a "Christian" life out of the fear of failure. We read our Bible in the morning, we pray, we witness, we do all of the holy behavioral things just so no one can consider us a failure as a Christian.

There is an interesting story told about the legendary football coach Paul "Bear" Bryant and a particular defensive backfield player on his team. This player was slow, but in one game an opposing running back got through the line and was running for a touchdown. It was the defensive player's responsibility to be the safety valve and to stop him. The ball carrier got past him by 10 or 15 yards, but suddenly this previously slow defensive back chased the speedy runner down and tackled him before he made the touchdown. Reporters gathered around this defensive back after the game and said, "That was amazing! You have never been known for your speed, and yet you ran that guy down and caught him. How did you do that?" He responded, "I play for Coach Bryant. That guy was only running for a touchdown — I was running for my life!"

Fear can be a powerful motivation, but there is only one fear that we should have in our lives — the fear of the Lord. If we just fear failure it may motivate us to get many things done, but we will not be doing God's will. We will be responsive to what we fear. We will only be able to hear God's voice clearly if He is the only One we fear. Any other fears in our life will just add static to our line of communication.

Another god that is prominent on the list is the fear of criticism. We may say. "I don't really care what people say," but we really do. If fear of criticism determines the actions that we take, then acceptance with man is a god. The apostle Paul said, "If I were still trying to please men, *I would not be a bond servant of Christ*" (Galatians 1:10). We cannot serve the Lord and be controlled by the fear of man at the same time. If we fear men then we have made men our gods too. Our God is a jealous God; He will not share our devotion with any other gods.

There may have been times when we knew we should take a stand on a certain issue on our job or in our community. Why didn't we? Usually because of the fear of criticism. Until that god is removed from our life, we will still have that spirit of fear ministering to us. As long as the spirit of fear is controlling us, the spirit of power, love and of a sound mind is not in control.

The fear of death can be another god in our life which possesses the power to corrupt us. Much of Satan's access to our life is through this powerful fear.

Remember the beer commercial: "You only go around once in life; you had better grab all the gusto you can." This was actually appealing to the fear of death in us. They recognized that the fear of death can be a powerful motivator. It can get middle-aged men and women to start thinking: "Hey, I'm not going to be here forever, and I haven't done everything yet." Men start thinking: "I've only had one wife, and death is right down the road. I better check it out. There may be some better women around." And they start thinking: "I've only had one job; I've only lived in one place," and the fear of death compels them do things they would never otherwise do, things which will in fact lead to death.

When we are afraid of death, life is our god. Life is a wonderful thing, but it is not good enough to be a god. There is only One good enough to be God. His name is Jesus.

How about sickness? Are we afraid of sickness? The spirit of failure and the spirit of sickness often work together. Some people can be healed of a disease but are so gripped with the fear of getting sick again that they soon lose their healing.

Some people fall into the trap of worshipping health when they start studying healing. They begin to make health a god and take the attitude that if you are healthy, nothing else matters. That too is a false god. Staying healthy is important, but if it becomes a god we will begin to fear sickness, which is to serve sickness, which will usually result in sickness. Health is not a worthy god, and the fear of sickness is not a spirit that should control you.

Another popular god is the fear of embarrassment, which is related to the fear of man. What is our god when we have the spirit of embarrassment? Propriety. It is amazing how many of us have propriety as a dominating attitude. We want everything to be accepted and approved. That is why the Lord sometimes has a hard time coming into our church service. We have an unconscious concept of how things are supposed to be in church. For example, an evangelical church is expected to be reverent. That being interpreted means *quiet*. There should not be a lot of activity. If some people begin praising God at the same time or saying things aloud, then the propriety is disturbed. And, yes, we believe in people being delivered from demonic powers, but not in our services. We believe in people being healed and saved, and it is all right for people to shout when they are being moved on by God, but not in our church. Let them do it where it would be proper.

You may think I am overemphasizing this point, but that is a real hindrance to the coming of God's presence. What is the problem? It's a the fear of embarrassment. Are you afraid that God is going to embarrass you? He will only if you are giving in to the god of propriety.

Wouldn't it be all right if Jesus did anything he wanted to do? Couldn't He do it in your church without your being embarrassed? Well, there were times when Jesus dealt with the demonic, with a paralytic, with the lame. There were times when he dealt with the lost, and times when he answered questions to those who would be critical. If Jesus' words or works would embarrass you in your church service, you are operating under a spirit of fear of embarrassment.

That is what happened to the Pharisees. When Jesus came into town with his triumphal entry and all the people were praising him with a loud voice, the Pharisees said: "Calm them down, Jesus, tell them to shut up; that is not the proper thing to do." And Jesus said, "Even the rocks will cry out if they are silent."

Another common fear is of financial trouble. What is the god behind this fear? Money. Financial stability is a wonderful thing to have; it certainly is not wrong. But when it becomes a dominating influence controlling our life, it becomes a god that we fear. We are then putting our faith in finances in place of the true God. That fear begins to work right then to control our life. Many people are motivated to get financially free, not so they can use their resources to the glory of God, but out of fear of financial trouble. Investments are made, savings accounts are started, principles of sound financial planning are carried out, not in submission to God or to glorify Him (though that will usually be our claim),but so they don't get into financial difficulty.

The most damaging fear among theologians (and of course, we are all theologians) is the fear of error. We are so afraid we will get into error that we will not be open to certain truths. At one point because several articles had appeared in major newspapers and denominational publications describing our ministry as a cult, I was praying, "Lord, I really don't think that's true. Obviously, I don't think we are any kind of cult. But I do want to make sure that we are in the truth. First, because only the true get to be free and I don't want to miss you. But, secondly, I don't want to get into error because some people listen to me, and I am not only responsible for myself but for them also. So please don't let me get into error."

As the Lord and I were discussing this, it was almost as if He spoke audibly to me, saying: "One of the reasons you have a tough time discovering truth is because you live under the impression that truth and error live on opposite sides of town. In fact, most of the time they are next door neighbors." I began to understand how true that is, how it is our tendency when we see error to run so far away from error that we move all the way to the other side of town. Then we live on that side of town, not because of we are seeking the truth but because we are running from error. This usually causes us to swing to the opposite doctrinal extreme that is often as far from the truth as the original error. We will never come to the truth because we fear error but because we love the truth.

Sometimes the devil is such a good counterfeiter that he can get his error right next door to the truth. I grew up with some influence of extreme Calvinism. This doctrine borders on fatalism, which is essentially the philosophy that "What is to be will be." Everything was decreed before we got here; our choices do not really matter. You are born to go to hell, or you are born to go to heaven. This implies that we can do whatever we want because everything is already decided. If that were right, then Paul wasted a lot of time telling us about our choices. I grew up knowing that fatalism was error, but I ran so far away from fatalism that I ran into an erroneous position of my own. I would hear people talking about predestination, election, foreknowledge and all those things, and it would make me angry.

One day while in seminary I was translating the book of Ephesians from Greek to English when it became apparent that the truth of the sovereignty of God lives right next door to the error of fatalism. If you run too far away from fatalism, you will run out of the neighborhood and miss one of the great truths, a truth that may give more peace and rest in your life than any other truth.

This also helped me to understand why some are calling others neo-gnostics today. Gnosticism is an error of the first century that included the belief that you had to have a secret knowledge to understand spiritual truths and that only the elite received it. Today there is such a fear of gnosticism among theologians, preachers and those who study the Scripture. Many have run so far away from it that they have rejected the possibility that a person can hear from God without everybody else hearing. But the Lord Himself stated the truth that only those who have ears will hear God, so in a sense there is a secret knowledge. But this truth and ability to hear from the Lord is available to anyone who is open to God.

When the seventy came back from the mission Jesus had sent them on and were excited because the demons were subject to them, Jesus said, "Rejoice that your names are written in heaven." But the Scripture says Jesus rejoiced in his spirit greatly to the Father and said, "Father, I thank you that you have hidden these things from the wise and intelligent and the prudent and you have revealed them unto babies." Is Jesus a neo-gnostic? Jesus is saying that He is giving the disciples knowledge and instruction that the rest are not receiving.

There is another error that arises from the fear of error: the error of the exaltation of the gifts of the Spirit. This consists of lifting up any one gift as the key to the whole Christian experience. Those who complain about people who exalt the gift of tongues usually exalt the gifts of teaching. The exaltation of any gift, saying that this gift is the one that releases all the power, has caused some people to run all the way to the other side of town, saying: "We don't believe in gifts, we don't need gifts, let's 'forbid not' but let's 'seek not'" (in other words, ignore). Those who exercise all the gifts and those who exalt them many times live next door. If you run too far from exaltation, you will run all the way from the exercising of gifts and miss the truth of God entirely.

Any church that is unwilling to exercise the gifts will never move into the power and the flow of God. You cannot do the works of God in the power of natural talents; it takes supernatural gifts, and they are all necessary. If we are not afraid of them, we will see how they fit into their proper categories and we will not be exalting any one gift or fearing any other. Some people fear the gift of tongues. If you are afraid of it, what spirit is ministering to you? It is obviously not a spirit of sound mind; it is a spirit of fear.

The error of perfectionism and the truth of imparted holiness live next door to one another. Once I and a few other friends were accused of preaching perfectionism. I asked Jack Taylor about it and he said, "I haven't met anybody close enough to perfection to discuss it." Neither had I. But it is an error to say that God does such a sanctifying work in your life that He eradicates the possibility of your making a choice toward evil. It is truth to say this: When Jesus saved you, He did more than change the books in heaven; He changed you; He made you holy. You are the righteousness of God in Christ Jesus. You are as righteous as Jesus is. It is not just imputed, not just legally on the books in heaven, but in reality you are righteous *in* Jesus.

That does not mean you cannot sin. It means you are free from sin. Those concepts live close together. If you are so afraid of the error that you don't ever get in the neighborhood, then you will miss one of the greatest truths in the Bible.

Then there are the miracle seekers; those who are always wanting to see a miracle are often failing to mature in the Word or in the Spirit. They go from one conference to another just looking for miracles. Even so, often these same people live right next door to those who have matured in the Spirit and walk in the Word to the degree that signs follow them. If you don't look carefully you will not know the difference between them.

Jesus said, "If you will go and just say my word — you don't have to explain it, illustrate it, soften it, work it around people's mental blocks, just go *say it* — I will work with you and these signs will follow." Searching through church history, I cannot find a time when the signs did not follow at least some of the disciples of Jesus. At times they were called weirdos, heretics and other names, but the signs of God followed them. There are still some today who are just simple enough in their faith to believe Jesus meant what He said, and signs and wonders follow them. Don't be guilty of saying they are miracle seekers until you know for certain. There are some miracle seekers who Jesus said only wanted to see a sign, and they were an evil and perverse generation. Even so, He said that signs follow those who follow Him. *There are those who follow signs and then there are those who are followed by signs.*

Can you see how easy it is to be so focused on error and guarding yourself from error that you miss truth? When you are afraid of error, that is your God — Truth as a position. Jesus said, "I am the truth." He is always to be our God, but not truth as a doctrine, a set of precepts, a dogma, or a theological position. If any of those is your god, the spirit of the fear of error is ruling in your life. That is why many people cannot move with God as he leads us in different directions and takes us to new places. They say. "I'm afraid we will get into error. I'm afraid we'll get into the Charismatic error, the Catholic error, the Presbyterian error." You don't have to be afraid of any error. Walk with Jesus and you will find that you are sometimes walking close to an error, but that is because error is often found living next door to truth. It is a high level strategy of the enemy to get his error as close to the truth as he can. Every time the Lord sows wheat, he comes along and sows tares *in the same field*.

If we are going to be controlled by the spirit of power, love and a sound mind, we must refuse to receive the spirit of fear. In order to refuse the spirit of fear we must receive the Holy Spirit to have power and a sound mind. The spirit of fear comes with idols, those gods that rule and reign in our life. As long as the spirit of fear is present, we cannot hear clearly. The most important thing in ministering in supernatural power is being able to hear God.

Chapter Six
. . . .

Authority And Power

In Luke 9:1-2 we read, "And He [Jesus] called the twelve together and gave them power and authority over **all** the demons, and to heal diseases. And He sent them out to proclaim the kingdom of God, and to perform healing."

One day it occurred to me just how big a risk the Lord had taken in doing this. He was entrusting His kingdom into some very shaky hands. These were the men who wanted to turn the Samaritans into charcoal briquettes because they were not following Jesus. They were the ones who saw someone else casting out demons after they had failed and told him to quit because he wasn't with their group. One of their major discussions had been on determining which of them was the greatest. Would you trust the proclaiming of your kingdom to some guys who sounded like wrestlers on Saturday afternoon television? Still, Jesus called them and gave them His ministry. "I want you to go and do what I have been doing," He said.

As I thought of the risk Jesus took in giving His ministry to such incompetent men, I was reminded that He had done the same thing with me! I wrote in the margin of my Bible,

"If Jesus risked His power with me, I am going to risk believing it; I'm going to use the power and authority that He gave me."

When we are about to pray for the sick or confront demonic powers, we are often confronted with the risk of failure and potential humiliation. We usually think, "What if I trust God and He doesn't do it?" "What if I go to perform His works and He doesn't show up?" There is no question that there is risk involved if we determine to minister as He has commanded us to, but I think that He is taking a whole lot more of a risk than we are! God is faithful; He will perform what He has declared in His word — we are the ones with the problems! If God Almighty will have that much faith in us shouldn't we have faith in Him?

Notice two words in this passage: "power" and "authority." Every disciple of Jesus has power and authority. They are part of the equipment that comes with the job. With that power and authority you can do anything Jesus tells you to do. In fact you can even do the same works He did — *and greater ones!* (John 14:12). The authority did not stop when the apostolic age ended; the Great Commission makes that clear. He said, "I want you to go into all the world, make disciples of all nations and teach them to observe everything I have taught you." What had he taught them? That they had power and authority to cast out all the demons, to perform healing and to preach the kingdom of God. We have not really made a disciple until we have taught them to believe all Jesus said *and to observe it.*

That word "observe" is important. We have taught people to believe, so we have people saying, "I believe every word in the Bible." But Jesus did not say to teach them to thump it and believe it, but to observe it — to *do* it! Was Jesus content to have His disciples just believe that they had the power to heal and to cast out demons and proclaim the kingdom of God? No — He made them do it. He watched them do it; He corrected them when they did not do it right. He made them produce. That is a true disciple. He later said that "A disciple is not above his teacher; but everyone *after he is fully trained will be like his teacher*" (Luke 6:40). If we are true disciples of Christ, being trained by Him, we will do the works that He did.

Why can so few Christians do the works that He did? Mostly because we do not understand much about authority and power. Where does authority reside? *In the name of JESUS!* Again, our Teacher said, "Verily, verily I say to you, he who believes in Me, the works that I do shall he do also; and greater works than these shall he do; because I go to the Father" (John 14:12). Then he tells us *how* to do it: "Whatever you ask in my name, that will I do that the Father may be glorified in the Son. If you ask anything in my name, I will do it." The name of Jesus is pretty powerful, isn't it?

In John 16:23-28 He says,

> And in that day you will ask Me no question. Truly, truly, I say to you, if you shall ask the Father for anything, He will give it to you in my name. Until now you have asked for nothing in My name; ask, and you will receive, that your joy may be full. These things I have spoken to you in figurative language; an hour is coming, when I will speak no more to you in figurative language, but will tell you plainly of the Father. In that day, you will ask in My name; and I do

not say to you that I will request the Father on your
behalf; for the Father himself loves you, because you
have loved Me, and have believed that I came forth
into the world; I am leaving the world again, and
going to the Father.

When you use the name of Jesus, you get the works that Jesus
did, if you believe in that name.

In the New Testament you find a teaching in the gospels,
an illustration of it in the book of Acts and the explanation of
it in the epistles. If we really believe the teaching, we will also
do the acts. After we have believed it and done it we will then
have the authority to teach it ourselves.

In Acts 3:6 a man sits by the Gate Beautiful, begging alms,
but Peter and John have no money to give him. So what did
they do? "But Peter said, 'I do not possess silver and gold,
but what I do have I give to you.'" What did he have? He had
authority. "In the name of Jesus Christ the Nazarene —
walk!" Healing was performed in that *name*. In verse 16, the
man is trying to tell what happened and some began to think
that Peter and John were something special. But Peter said,
"We are nothing; let me explain what happened. On the basis
of faith in His name, it is the name of Jesus which has
strengthened this man whom you see and know."

Acts 4:12 says: "And there is salvation in no one else; for
there is no other name under heaven that has been given
among men by which we must be saved." The chief priest
didn't like what Peter, John and the other disciples were
doing and they commanded them to stop because their
works were too extraordinary and miraculous. Here is the
command they gave them (Acts 4:17): "But in order that it

may not spread any further among the people, let us warn them to speak no more to any man in this name."

What was the response of the disciples to this threat? "And now, Lord, take note of their threats, and grant that thy bond servants may speak Thy word with all confidence, while Thou dost extend Thy hand to heal, and signs and wonders take place through the name of Thy holy servant Jesus" (Acts 4:29-30). We see here that the disciples *expected* healings, signs and wonders to take place when they spoke in the name of Jesus.

In the next chapter we find the disciples being upbraided again by members of the religious community because of the miraculous works they were doing. Arresting officers had brought them before the Council, and the high priest questioned them, saying:

> We gave you strict orders not to continue teaching in this name, and behold, you have filled Jerusalem with your teaching, and intend to bring this man's blood upon us (Acts 5:28).

Wouldn't it be marvelous if all teachers today taught in Jesus' name, rather than teaching in their own authority, wisdom and intellect? When you teach in Jesus' name, it has the same effect as when Jesus taught. In verse 41 of the same chapter we see that "they went on their way from the presence of the Council, rejoicing that they had been considered worthy to suffer shame for His name." His name was so wonderful, so powerful, so important to them in getting the works of God done, that they were honored to suffer for it.

Philip was not an apostle, prophet or evangelist in the strict sense of the word. In modern terms he was just a layman. He was only a deacon, but when he went to the city of Samaria preaching, the entire city was stirred and gave him their attention. Why? "The multitudes with one accord were giving attention to what was said by Philip, *as they heard and saw the signs which he was performing*" (Acts 8:6). What was Philip doing to perform these signs? "But when they believed Philip *preaching the good news about the kingdom of God and the name of Jesus Christ*, they were being baptized, men and women alike" (Acts 8:12). He simply preached about the kingdom of God and the name of Jesus.

When God chose Saul of Tarsus who was to become the most renowned of the apostles, notice how God defined his ministry: "But the Lord said to him, [Ananias] 'Go, for he is a chosen instrument of Mine, *to bear My name* before the Gentiles and kings and the sons of Israel; for I will show him how much he must suffer for my name's sake'" (Acts 9:15-16). Paul was called to bear the Lord's name and to suffer for the sake of that name. Everything that Paul later did with supernatural power he did in His name.

> But Barnabus took hold of him and brought him to
> the apostles and described to them how he had seen
> the Lord on the road, and that he had talked to him,
> and how at Damascus he had spoken out boldly *in
> the name of Jesus.* (Acts 9:27)

You will get God's explanation of why He called you out in Acts 15. The Jerusalem Council is in progress and Simeon is speaking. Simeon has related how God first concerned

Himself about taking from among the Gentiles a people for His name. The purpose of your call: to represent His name.

In Acts 19:11, Paul was using the name of Jesus so authoritatively that the demons were leaving immediately. The Jewish exorcists, those who used incantations and formulas to try to cast out demons, observed Paul doing it just by using the name of Jesus. So they said, "Hey, that's a better way," and decided to copy his method. They began by saying, "In the name of Jesus whom Paul preaches, come out." And the demons said, "We know Jesus and we know Paul, but who are you?" They jumped out on the exorcists, beat them and tore their clothes off. Verse 17 says:

> And this became known to all, both Jews and Greeks, who lived in Ephesus: and fear fell upon them all and *the name of the Lord Jesus* was being magnified.

It is not by just expressing the syllables J-E-S-U-S that gives the authority. Remember Luke 9:1 — *He gave them authority.* Neither is it the volume with which we use His name, or any other formula — *it is who gave the authority that makes His name effective!* Every Christian has the authority to use the name of Jesus, but it is not made effective by a certain formula or procedure, but by the One who gave it, the One whose name we are using. Our faith is in the authority of Jesus, not just a method.

We must recognize that we do need the power and authority to accomplish what He has sent us to do in His name. There is a story about a tavern owner who had a big drunk tearing his place apart. A police officer was sent to take care of the situation. He was a little man with a big badge on his chest. He walked in and said, "In the name of the state, I command you to cease and desist; you are under arrest." At that, the big drunk backhanded him over the bar and into the wall. The officer had all the authority of the state, but he was not able to get the job done. Another policeman was sent down. He had his little badge and uniform on too, and he went in and said with a loud voice: "I command you to cease and desist; you are under arrest by the authority of the state." The drunk backhanded him across the bar and into the wall. He had plenty of authority and volume but he didn't get the job done either. A third policeman was sent. He was 6'7" and weighed 275 lbs. He walked in and said, "In the name of the law of this state, I arrest you." The big drunk started to take a swing at him, but the officer put a bear hug on him, subdued him and dragged him off to jail. He not only had authority, but he also had the power.

Jesus did not just give us legal authority; He gave us power too. Many times we have tried to operate in our legal authority by using the name of Jesus with no experiential power of the Holy Spirit, and we did not get the job done. We must have both.

We understand that the authority comes from the Lord but how do we get the power that we need? In Matthew 3:11 John the Baptist declares, "As for me, I baptize you in water for repentance, but He who is coming after me is mightier than I, and I am not fit to remove His sandals; He Himself will baptize you with the Holy Spirit and fire." John is saying that a time will come when you will be baptized in the Holy Spirit and with fire. Jesus gave the definition of that ex-perience in Acts 1:4-5 & 8:

And gathering them together, He commanded them not to leave Jerusalem, but to wait for what the Father had promised, 'Which,' He said, 'you heard of from Me; for John baptized with water, but you shall be baptized with the Holy Spirit not many days from now ... But you shall receive power [not authority; they already had authority] when the Holy Spirit has come upon you; and you shall be My witnesses both in Jerusalem, and in all Judea and Samaria, and even to the remotest part of the earth.

Don't worry about the semantics of the baptism of the Holy Spirit — *just get it!* We need it to accomplish the mandate that he has given to us as Christians or he would not have put such an emphasis on it. When you get it you will not be so concerned with "wrangling about words."

How is the gospel to be preached? Paul summarized it in I Corinthians 2:1-4:

And when I came to you, brethren, I did not come with superiority of speech or of wisdom, proclaiming to you the testimony of God. For I determined to know nothing among you except Jesus Christ, and Him crucified. And I was with you in weakness and in fear and in much trembling. And my message and my preaching were not in persuasive words of wisdom, but *in demonstration of the Spirit and of power.*

Much of the preaching of the gospel today is not in the demonstration of power. What we consider power is when someone gets up and yells and sweats and makes us cry and laugh and gets people to come down the aisles. That is not a demonstration of *the Spirit* and power; that is a demonstration of *flesh* and its power. When we minister by the Holy Spirit Who was sent to testify of Jesus, He will work through us the very works that Jesus did.

The gospel that is generally preached in America will work in no other place in the world but in America (if it is working here). If you go to Africa, India or almost any other part of the world, and you preach a Jesus who cannot do what He did in the New Testament, they simply will not believe you; their gods can do better than that. They are not interested in a cerebral Jesus. If He cannot heal, deliver, save and do the miraculous, they do not want Him because their gods can do those things. If you tell them about Jesus, it confuses them when you say: "Now the Jesus we are telling you about is the Jesus who cast out demons, healed the sick, saved people and performed miracles, but He does not do that today. That was back in the days of the disciples. He will not do that, but you need to trust Him anyway because He can save you from sin and take you to heaven instead of hell." That Gospel will not work any place else but in America because it is cerebral. We only accept it in America because we have been conditioned by Madison Avenue to accept the things that have style more than the things which have substance. This causes us to believe with our minds instead of our hearts, but as the apostle Paul declared to the Romans who were likewise inclined: "For with the *heart* man believes resulting in righteousness" (Romans 10:10). Only that which is spirit can touch man's spirit; that is why we must preach with "demonstrations of the Spirit and power."

After Paul said that the Gospel he preached was in the demonstration of power and of the Spirit, he explains why in I Corinthians 2:5: "That your faith should not rest on the wisdom of men, but on the power of God." When someone has been won by the real gospel preached in the power of the Holy Spirit, you do not have to labor nearly as hard to keep them from backsliding or drifting away from the Lord, because their faith will rest on the power of God instead of mere human props and effort.

Paul elaborates on this principle in Romans 15:18-19:

> For I will not presume to speak of anything except what Christ has accomplished through me, resulting in the obedience of the Gentiles by word or deed. [By word and deed. They are not only believing the Word of God; they are performing it; they are doing it.] In the power of signs and wonders, in the power of the Spirit; so that from Jerusalem and round about as far as Illyricum I have fully preached the gospel of Christ.

The Gentiles had so received the gospel of power that it was producing in them the work of Jesus. They were believing and working. They were doing the works of Jesus. If Jesus really is "the same yesterday, today and forever" can we not expect the same from Him today?

If so, how are we going to live in this power? How do you know when you are operating in this power? When you are operating in the power of the Holy Spirit you will see that power released in the Church through the gifts of the Spirit. That is one of the reasons why the devil makes such a controversy over the gifts. If we are afraid of the gifts we never move into the expression and the reality of the power and therefore cannot carry out our authority. The Lord intended for us to receive all the gifts. In I Corinthians 12: 4-11, He says:

> Now there are varieties of gifts, but the same Spirit. And there are varieties of ministries, but the same Lord. And there are varieties of effects, but the same God who works all things in all persons. But to each one is given the manifestation [or the demonstration?] of the Spirit for the common good. For to one is given the word of wisdom through the Spirit, and to another the word of knowledge according to the same Spirit; to another faith by the same Spirit, and to another, gifts of healing by the one Spirit, And to another the effecting of miracles, and to another prophecy, and to another the distinguishing of spirits, to another various kinds of tongues, and to another the interpretation of tongues. But one and the same spirit works all these things, distributing to each individually just as He wills.

Here is what happens in the demonstration of the Spirit and power. When a person is willing to walk in the power of the Holy Spirit, he has received the release of power in his being. You may call that the baptism, the filling, the anointing or whatever you like.

The fact is that you receive the Holy Spirit when you are saved. It is by reception of the Holy Spirit that we are regenerated, born again, baptized into the Body of Christ. That happens at conversion, but there are many times when we need the filling of the Holy Spirit, that the fruit of the Spirit will be produced in our lives. The filling of the Holy Spirit is primarily for character. It enables us to live above circumstances and produce the character of Jesus.

But the day comes in our lives — it could happen at conversion, but for most of us it does not — when we realize we have been commissioned by Jesus to express Him on this earth. We are to do His works here. We are not just to be good, loving, kind, patient, long-suffering people, but we are to do His works. Hungry people, crippled people, bound people, blind people and lost people are everywhere, and we have been commissioned to do the works of Jesus with them. We realize that our talents are not enough. We have tried that, attempted to do it with persuasive speech, education and everything at our command, but it is not working. We realize we need more of what He demonstrated in His personal ministry. Then we may realize that He has already given us the power of the Holy Spirit, but that power must be appropriated.

Many times that is a wonderful experience — an experience subsequent to conversion that is an experience of joy, of release, of power. I like to describe it as an anointing because the word "anointing" is used several times to describe the nature of the Spirit.

When you are willing to come to that realization and by faith receive what is already yours, because He is already resident in you, the power of the Holy Spirit that has been lying dormant is released. When that power is released in you, so is the demonstration or manifestation of that power. He begins to manifest Himself through you in these different effects or manifestations. The gifts of the Spirit are listed in I Corinthians 12:8-11. They are: *a word of wisdom, the word of knowledge, faith, gifts of healing, miracles, prophecy, discerning of spirits, various kinds of tongues (or languages) and interpretation of tongues.* Let's look at each of these briefly.

The first gift listed is called *a word of wisdom.* This is not just having wisdom, but is a supernatural wisdom that goes beyond human abilities. It is a special insight into the mind and purpose of God. A good Biblical demonstration of this is when Jesus was confronted by the situation of the woman caught in adultery. What looked like a sure theological trap was unraveled by His simple but profound wisdom when He stated, "Let the one who is without sin among you cast the first stone." When we too are caught in such circumstances that are beyond our ability and wisdom to deal with, we need to learn to turn to the Lord and seek His wisdom — even in situations where it is needed spontaneously.

The gift of a *word of knowledge* is the ability to know facts that you could not know without God telling you. You might say it is knowing intuitively, but it is more than that — it is revelation from the Lord. Peter had received a word of knowledge when he declared that Jesus was the Christ, the Son of God. The Lord explained to Peter that this had not been revealed to him by flesh and blood but by the Father (see Matthew 16:16-17). We also see the Lord Jesus demonstrating this gift in His encounter with the woman at the well when He told her how many husbands she had. We need to have the gift of a word of wisdom working with the gift of a word of knowledge so that we will know how to apply it properly. How many of us, having understood the adultery of the woman at the well, would not have just clobbered her with that knowledge? Jesus used the knowledge to gently lead her to salvation.

The *gift of faith* is more than just having faith. Just as the gift of healing is given to heal others, the gift of faith is given so that we can impart faith to others. It is a supernatural impartation that is more than just giving someone encouragement. Just as the gifts of a word of wisdom and a word of knowledge often work together, the gift of faith often works together with the gifts of healing and miracles.

The *gifts of healing* and *miracles* are similar but are not the same. The gift of healing operates to heal anything from the flu to cancer or AIDS. This healing may be instantaneous or it may take a period of time, but regardless it is God doing a supernatural work to reverse an affliction. Some people also attribute the deliverance from mental afflictions to the gift of healing. The gift of miracles tends to be more spectacular and is usually creative in nature, such as the straightening of deformed limbs, giving sight to one who is born blind, etc.

The *gift of prophecy* is in some ways like the gift of a word of knowledge, but it is usually related to knowing details about the future. This gift can relate to international events or to personal ones, like the words that had been given to Timothy, with which Paul urged him to use to "fight the good fight" (see I Timothy 1:18). This gift was obviously also used to impart a spiritual gift to him (see I Timothy 4:14). The Lord Jesus was operating in the gift of prophecy when He foretold His own crucifixion, how Judas would betray Him and Peter would deny Him, as well as when He was foretelling events concerning the end of the age.

Discerning of spirits is likewise a supernatural gift. We see the Lord Jesus demonstrating this gift on numerous occasions. Paul also demonstrated it at times such as when he cast out the "spirit of divination" from the servant girl (see Acts 16:16-18). Paul did not address the girl, but he "turned and said to the spirit" (verse 18). With the dramatic increase of Satanic worship and cult activity throughout the world, we desperately need this gift operating in the Body of Christ. The Lord has given us authority over unclean spirits, but we need to know what we are boxing so that we are not just beating the air.

The *gifts of tongues and interpretation of tongues* are likewise important gifts for the building up of the church. The Holy Spirit does not impart gifts that do not have a purpose. Even though the enemy has tried to use these gifts to bring division in the church, their actual purpose is to bring unity. They were given as a sign that the church is to be the antithesis to the Tower of Babel where men's languages were scattered. On the Day of Pentecost, when this gift was first given to the church, all of the different worshippers in Jerusalem, who had come from many different nations and had different languages, were all able to understand the utterances given by the disciples through this gift. The gift of tongues is a supernatural gift that imparts a spiritual understanding which transcends our natural minds. This gift begins to open the hearts of believers to the language of the spirit that cannot be understood by "a natural man" (see I Corinthians 2:11-16). The gift of interpretation of tongues is given to bridge that which is spoken by the Spirit and that which must be understood by the mind.

There are those who say that if you ever have the experience of baptism or anointing of the Spirit, you will speak in tongues. I do not think that is true. I think some people do speak in tongues when they have that experience, but when you are willing to move into that power and realm of ministry, you can expect one or more of these manifestations to start happening in your life. I personally think it is erroneous to say that it would always be tongues or any of the other gifts. You can find Biblical evidence that different things happened. But there is a release in a whole new realm of authority and power to minister. We can see examples of it in Acts.

Let us look again at what happened at Pentecost. The occurrence begins with Acts 2:1: "And when the day of Pentecost had come, they were all together in one place. And suddenly there came from heaven a noise *like* a violent, rushing wind..." They did not say a wind came, but a noise like a violent, rushing wind. This is noteworthy, because at a James Robison Bible Conference in the early 1980s, a number of people came to us saying, "Did you hear the wind last night?" I did not hear any wind. One man said he heard the sound of the wind very strongly. What had happened was that in the service all pastors had been invited to come to the front. Several hundred pastors came and they were praying and repenting before God. The man said he thought the noise was made by all those preachers groaning and repenting. But as he began to walk around the building, he could not determine the source of the sound. Some people from our church told us they heard the same sound, the sound of a wind. I have never heard that sound, but I have encountered several people around the country who have been in the presence of God in certain situations and have heard the sound of a wind. To one lady, it was so real that she looked at her husband, and asked, "Is my hair blowing?" He said, "No, your hair is not blowing." She said, "Well, listen to all that wind." But there was no wind.

Resuming at verse 3: "And there appeared to them tongues as of fire distributing themselves, and they rested on each one of them. And they were all filled with the Holy Spirit and began to speak with other tongues, as the Spirit was giving them utterance."

We can debate about whether it was a known language or an unknown language, but it definitely was a supernatural phenomenon. So we see here one of the demonstrations of the Spirit was the phenomenon of speaking in a language unknown to the speaker, whether or not it was unknown to all mankind. Thus, tongues was one of the manifestations of the release of power.

Now go on to verse six: "And when this sound occurred, the multitude came together, and were bewildered, because they were each one hearing them speak in his own language." This is the manifestation of the interpretation of tongues. It happened to the individual listener. Each is hearing in his own language.

Then, in verses 14-16, right in the middle of this demonstration of power, we see a prophecy:

> But Peter, taking his stand with the eleven, raised his voice and declared to them: 'Men of Judea, and all of you who live in Jerusalem, let this be known to you, and give heed to my words. These men are not drunk, as you suppose, for it is only the third hour of the day: but this is that which was spoken of through the prophet Joel.'

And Peter begins to take the word of God and prophesy. So we also see prophecy occurring as a demonstration of the power of the Holy Spirit.

Acts 3:1-11 records an incident in which Peter and John go by the gate of the Temple and see the man who was crippled and asking for alms. Suddenly, they said, "In the name of Jesus Christ the Nazarene, stand up and walk." This is a demonstration not only of authority used in the name of Jesus, but a demonstration of power. It could be seen as a demonstration of healing, miracles or faith. I personally believe it is a demonstration of two: healing and miracles. The man was healed, but when the incident is referred to later, it is called a miracle.

Acts 4:19 presents another demonstration of the Spirit's power as released through a word of wisdom. The Council is questioning Peter and John and they say to them: "You cannot speak any more in Jesus' name." The disciples have a sticky problem. They know they are supposed to be submissive to the godly ordained authorities, and yet they also know they have to be obedient to Jesus. Through mere human knowledge, it is hard to determine what to do. So they need supernatural wisdom. Verse 19 says:

> But Peter and John answered and said to them, 'Whether it is right in the sight of God to give heed to you rather than to God, you be the judge. For we cannot stop speaking what we have seen and heard.'

That is a word of wisdom. That is wisdom they received on the spot. It is situational; they did not have it before they arrived; they had not studied it through. God told them on the spot through a word of wisdom.

It is in verse 16 that the healing of the crippled man is identified as a miracle: The council said, "What shall we do with these men? For the fact that a noteworthy miracle has taken place through them is apparent to all who live in Jerusalem." So we see here a miracle as a manifestation of power.

In verse 23 and following, the disciples were being beaten and persecuted. They began to pray and ask God to do signs and wonders through His name. They had confidence. In this we see a demonstration of faith.

Acts 5:1-10 gives the account of Sapphira telling a lie. All believers were selling their property and bringing the money to the apostles. Ananias and Sapphira brought a portion of their money and pretended to be giving the whole amount. In verse 3, Peter says: "Ananias, why has Satan filled your heart to lie to the Holy Spirit, and to keep back part of the price of the land?" How did Peter know that? By a word of knowledge. Peter received information on the spot that could not have been based on previous knowledge. He knew something that God told him at the moment. That is a word of knowledge, one of the manifestations of the power of the Spirit.

Look at verse 16: "And also the people from the cities in the vicinity of Jerusalem were coming together, bringing people who were sick or afflicted with unclean spirits; and they were all being healed." This is a manifestation of the discerning of spirits. People were coming with all kinds of spirits, and they had to know which were unclean spirits and which were not.

Clearly, members of the early Church operated not only in authority but in power. Their power was manifested not just in tongues, miracles or healings alone, but in all these things. If we are to operate today as the ministers of Jesus and do the work Jesus has told us to do, we must operate in both authority and power.

John Wimber describes the "manifestation," as "the dancing hand of God." If we are open to the Spirit of God as we meet together, realizing that we have the responsibility and the capability to minister, God's hand will dance on different ones. One person will receive one gift and another person another gift, and the glory of God will dance around. That is why it is important to have Body ministry. When we start operating in this spiritual realm, we will cut out much one-on-one counseling in which the staff has to do all the ministering. The reason is that when you are open to authority and power, the hand of God may rest on you and you will minister to the people around you, and somebody else may also minister to them. The hand of God may come on you to minister today, and it may not be on you tomorrow; it may be on someone else. But there will always be the ministry of God dancing around in the group.

What prevents us from operating in authority and power today, receiving and releasing the manifestation of the Holy Spirit? There are three basic reasons.

One reason that often stops us is fear of whatever manifestation God might want to demonstrate through us. We say:

"Wait a minute, Lord; I don't mind certain manifestations on me, but there are some I don't want." That is fear of the package. I do not think many believers are afraid of the Holy Spirit in His essence, but we may be afraid of the package we have seen Him in. We may have seen bad models from those who acted a little strange, and said, "Lord, if that is what I've got to do, forget it!" Because of a bad package, you are rejecting a gift. We must learn to distinguish the gift itself from the package that it sometimes comes in. Let us also understand that God sometimes purposely uses the "foolish things to confound those who are wise" (I Corinthians 1:27).

Prophecy does not have to come in King James English. At the close of a Bible conference session a man gave probably the most powerful prophecy I have ever heard in King James English and in what some would call the Pentecostal style. It came wrapped in that particular package. Later, another man coming from a different church background shared with James Robison, Jim Hylton and me almost exactly the same prophecy, but he did not use King James English or stand before the whole crowd. He handed it to us on a piece of paper. Two different packages, the same gift. You may say, "I like the second package better." Would you be willing to let God decide what package He puts it in? And would you not reject people who package things differently from what you prefer or expect?

Some people mess up the packaging. A man told me of someone who prophesied, saying: "Hear ye, hear ye: thus saith the Lord: 'I know you're scared; sometimes I get scared myself.'" I am not sure God said exactly that. (It does not give me much comfort!) If God has been scared, we are in trouble.

Some of us would tend to feel that since that was not a word straight from God, that prophecy is out. But the abuse of a gift does not negate the validity of the gift. That is like saying that because people abuse automobiles, you don't believe in automobiles. People have abused tongues, prophecy, healing and teaching. All the gifts have been abused. Do not negate a gift because someone has abused it. Many have abused Christianity itself but that does not negate the faith.

I have even heard people say, "Paul did not esteem tongues very highly, because he wrote to the Corinthians and told them to quit speaking as they were." But he did not say the gift was not real. He said they were abusing it, and he was correcting the abuse, not negating the validity of the gift. It is not wise to belittle anything that the Holy Spirit gives, and He is the One who gave the gift of tongues.

Again, one primary reason why we have trouble receiving the whole ministry of the Holy Spirit is because we've seen it packaged in some ways we don't like, and we are rejecting the packaging and missing the gift.

Another reason why we do not receive the manifestation is because of unresolved guilt. If you have unresolved guilt and you are unwilling to come to Jesus to be cleansed and to recognize your righteousness in Him, you will never be able to receive the whole ministry of the power of the Holy Spirit.

Another very obvious reason for not receiving the gifts of the Spirit is unbelief — just not being willing to believe that the power is available, that God is willing to give it to you, and that it is yours. You may think that you have to earn it or try to get holy enough to receive it. How holy do you have to get to be powerful? Holiness is a gift. Jesus said. "You will receive the gift of the Holy Spirit." He *gave* the disciples authority and power — they did not earn it.

Now that you have the gift of the Holy Spirit, appropriate it, receive it. You may wonder how you can receive the Holy Spirit if you already received Him when you were saved, but need to receive Him again. It is common practice among us to receive someone again and again. You probably have had to receive your husband or wife several times. You received them, but then on certain occasions you rejected them. After you reject someone, you have to receive them again. You do not have to get married all over again when you reject your husband or wife, but there has to be another appropriation of what is already yours.

I am convinced that many of us have not yet moved into that realm of ministry of authority and power because we have not received. We have fought in our minds against the "second blessing." If you need a second blessing, get a second one. If you need a third, get it. The hour is too late and the issue too important to let semantics confuse or frighten us. If you are not operating in authority and power, you might be better off to change your terminology. You must come to the place of realizing God has commissioned you to be a disciple. He commissioned you to do His work. His work is the work of preaching the gospel to the poor, healing the broken-hearted, setting the captives free, giving sight to the blind, releasing those who are bound, and preaching the acceptable year of the Lord. That means actually meeting the needs of the people, whatever they are. It does not mean just getting them into church, going good and doing better. That is not

His work. His work is changing people, and if you do not have the power and authority to do that you are lacking something.

"Well, I'm just not holy enough yet," you say: "I need a few more years of holiness." That is why we started this study in Luke 9. Those disciples were not exactly on the peak of maturity, but they were willing to receive what Jesus gave them — authority and power — and they were able to go out and perform the works of Jesus. You do not become mature before you begin to exercise your power and authority. You mature as you do it. None of us is as mature as we are going to be. You will never be as mature as you could be unless you get involved in doing the Word of God.

Jesus said go out and do it. Go out and preach the gospel. Go out and heal. Go out and pray for the sick. Go out and cast out demons. And what have we been guilty of doing? Calling in the specialist. When we have people who are troubled by the demonic, we call in a specialist. But you have a Specialist living in you. He gave you authority over all the demons and He gave you the power to use your authority.

When you get honest enough and desperate enough to say, "All right, I'm ready," God will start doing something. I had a precious experience not long ago. One of my best friends, the pastor of a little church in Alabama, was riding with me down the highway. He is a fast repenter. He is the type of person who believes strongly in what he believes, but if you show him he is wrong, he will say, "OK," and he will repent. He said he did not believe in a "second blessing." I told him basically what I have shared with you. I said that we could have recognized it and appropriated all the power of the Holy Spirit at conversion, but some of us have to get out in the ministry for a while and see the serious responsibility of meeting people's needs in the supernatural. When we realize we do not have the capacity to do it and see how desperately we need supernatural power, we appropriate what is already ours in the Holy Spirit, and the gifts and the power are released in us and we can help people.

Big tears began to run down this pastor's cheeks, and he said: "I don't know exactly what you call all that, but I know that is what I need," and he pulled over to the edge of the freeway. I said: "What are you going to do?" and he said: "I want you to pray for me and to lay your hands on me and ask God to release all that in me. Whatever it takes; I don't care. God can give me any gift He wants to. I'll receive them. I am unwilling any longer to go on trying to help people, but not having the ability to do so." I laid hands on him and prayed for him, and the power of God flooded his soul. Then we began hugging each other, praising God and shouting. There is no telling what the people driving by thought about us.

I got a letter from him a few weeks later, and he said there had been a marked difference in his life. First, there was the unusual love flowing out of him. You can't receive a baptism of power without the baptism of love. He said he had noticed that the gifts of God had been quickened within him and he was able to help others.

Would you like to have that? Jesus said: "I give you authority and power. Cast out all demons. Perform healing. Preach the kingdom of God." The authority is something you already have. It is a legal thing. You do not have to ask for it, or earn it, or be holy enough to have it. It is already yours. You received it when you received the name of Jesus. The reason it does not work much of the time is because we are not walking in the power that energizes it. And that power is released by the Holy Spirit in you, when you are willing to receive.

Chapter Seven

Faith Working Through Love

Not long ago I heard a man say: "When I signed up to be one of Jesus' disciples, I thought it was going to be like it was in the New Testament. But when I got in they told me I was supposed to be religious and I was terribly disappointed." It was a few years later before he discovered that he really could live the way he had signed up to live.

You can live that way, but to do so you have to be a part of the radical band of Christians whom Jesus calls disciples. Those who live in the supernatural are those who are willing to get out and do the work, not just talk about it. Many people are convinced that maturing spiritually and pleasing God is based on the amount of truth they acquire. These become bent on hearing more truth and learning new ways of saying it and organizing it. What God wants is for us to get just get active in doing the Word. We should quit saying that we believe it if we are not doing it. It is time to quit going to church and start being the church.

We will find no lack of opportunity to do the Word. There are sick people everywhere. We do not have to wait until the pastor calls the elders together. There are needy people everywhere with broken hearts and injured spirits. They are offended and usually cannot hear God, but Jesus came to heal broken hearts. As He is, so also are you in this world. We must learn to heal them as He did.

Some are captured by the enemy. Some have demonic depressions or affliction. We must deliver them. We do not have to wait until we get to Church to do it — we are the Church!

One problem is that we are afraid it will not work if we try it — but it will never work if we do not try it! Jesus gives us the whole picture in Mark 16: (This is after the resurrection):

> And after that, He appeared in a different form to two of them while they were walking along on their way to the country. And they went away and reported it to the others, but they did not believe them either.

Can you believe that people had trouble believing the resurrection of Jesus? The account continues:

> And afterward He appeared to the eleven themselves as they were reclining at table; and He reproached them for their unbelief and hardness of heart because they had not believed those who had seen Him after He had risen.

Unbelief has always been a problem, hasn't it? Here are the eleven still having a problem believing it. How did the Lord deal with their unbelief?

> And He said to them, 'Go into all the world and preach the Gospel to all creation. He who has

believed and has been baptized shall be saved; but he who has disbelieved shall be condemned. And these signs will accompany those who have believed. In My name they will cast out demons, they will speak with new tongues; they will pick up serpents, and if they drink any deadly poison, it shall not hurt them; they will lay hands on the sick, and they will recover.' So then, when the Lord Jesus had spoken to them, He was received up into heaven, and sat down at the right hand of God. And they went out and preached everywhere, while the Lord worked with them, and confirmed the word by the signs that followed.

Notice that as they were faithful to the Word, Jesus was faithful to do the signs. You do not have to worry about the signs if you will be faithful to the Word. This passage has evoked a lot of fear, because people are afraid of those who pick up snakes. Obviously, Jesus is not talking here about the presumption of trying to prove to God that you believe by demonstrating that you can pick up a snake. But in the book of Acts you will find what He said here actually happened. They cast out demons and spoke in new tongues. Paul was warming his hands by a fire, a poisonous snake bit him, and he flung it off into the fire and was not harmed. They laid hands on the sick, and they recovered. Those signs do follow disciples, and they still follow them today.

I heard Arthur Blessitt telling about walking over 21,000 miles carrying a cross around the world. He has spoken to the great dignitaries of the world and won tens of thousands of people to Jesus. He has walked through countries where the water was green and slimy and filled with wiggly things. When no clean water was available, Arthur would dip a cup into the infested water and say, "In the name of Jesus, I ask you to kill them all." He has never been sick one day, never had diarrhea or any amoebic problems. He is a living example that when you follow Jesus these signs will follow. Arthur does not get a cup of water filled with wiggly organisms to go before a congregation and say: "I want to prove to you it works." That would be presumption. But when he has to drink such things to do what God had called him to do, it really does work.

Notice when the signs start following: not while you are sitting in church listening to new teachings, not while you are going to another conference, not while you are in a Jerusalem conference discussing and analyzing the truth. No, the signs follow when you get out and begin proclaiming and doing the work of God. If we are not seeing the signs, it is because we are not doing the work.

Continuing our discussion of power and authority, consider the track on which power and authority runs. This is important because many people have gotten the power and authority, run off the track and gotten into serious trouble. There is a particular track, a particular road, upon which the power and authority must operate. In Galatians 5:6 we see: "For in Christ Jesus neither circumcision nor uncircumcision means anything, but *faith working through love.*" It is neither baptism nor non-baptism, closed communion in the Lord's Supper or open communion — it is not an issue of which rules we are complying with — the issue is "faith working through love."

Faith is an important aspect of life. Without faith you cannot please God and will not do the works of God. But faith only works through love. When the track of divine love is absent, there will be no track of divine power. Many have a real problem today with divine love because they try to develop it rather than receive it. Divine love is no more developed than is divine patience. You cannot develop divine patience; you can only receive it. All of these resources are gifts. Someday we may wake up to the fact that everything we get from God we get by receiving. You do not get anything from God by developing it and that includes love. When you receive it, you can give it.

Observe the disciples as they received power and authority. We also can become able ministers of the Word so that we can go out and do the works of Jesus, not just in the church but everywhere.

Wouldn't it be wonderful if there were two thousand people penetrating your city every day in the confidence that they could express Jesus anywhere they went — that if they came upon a person with a demonic problem they could deal with it or if they encountered people with physical or emotional problems they could deal with them? Do you realize what size building you would need to house people the way we structure church today in order to get everyone in once a week to worship, even if only half of us believed we could do it and got out and did it? You would have so many people you could not house them. That is the kind of Church God is trying to raise up today. It is no longer going to be the superstar church. It is going to be an "all saints cast." God is no longer going to share His glory with big preachers who have charisma, power and organizing ability. He is building a Church whose every member has authority and power and is doing the work of Jesus.

In Luke 9:1 and following, Jesus is equipping the disciples to do His work:

> And He called the twelve together, and gave them power and authority over all the demons, and to heal diseases. And He sent them out to proclaim the kingdom of God and to perform healing.

One day we too may learn what to preach and we too will preach the kingdom of God and perform healing. Evidently, the disciples believed in it because verse 6 says: "And departing, they began going about among the villages, preaching the gospel, and healing everywhere." Verse 11 continues:

> But the multitudes were aware of this and followed Him; and welcoming them, He began speaking to them about the kingdom of God and curing those who had need of healing.

It seems that Jesus is interested in the whole person, doesn't it? He didn't just preach to them — He met their needs. But notice the equipment that these disciples had: they had power and authority over all demons and all diseases, and they had the power to preach the kingdom of God.

In the next story, beginning in verse 12, Jesus illustrates something of great importance to them.

> And the day began to decline, and the twelve came and said to Him, 'Send the multitude away, that they may go into the surrounding villages and country-side and find lodging and get something to eat; for

here we are in a desolate place.' But He said to them,
'You give them something to eat!' ...

That is exactly what the Lord has done to us. We look
around at captive, blind and hurting people and we go to
God and say: "God, look at them. They hang out in bars and
nightclubs for acceptance. Their marriages are falling apart.
They are going to psychiatrists and medical specialists of all
kinds. They are on drugs. They fight addictions. God, help.
Do something. Feed them." But Jesus said: "I have a better
idea. *You feed them.*"

"Wait a minute, Lord," we protest. "I'm just a sinner saved
by grace, you know. I can't do much, Lord. I'm just one
beggar telling another beggar where I found some bread."
With that kind of concept, no wonder we cannot help the
dying world. The crowd will starve to death. He said, "You
feed them."

Behaving as we normally do, the disciples fell back on
their own resources and said: "Well, if we have to feed them,
how much do we have here?" They found five pieces of bread
and two fish. They probably thought they would look pretty
foolish trying to feed five thousand men and their families
with five pieces of bread and two fish, though not as foolish
as we look trying to feed people with our education, religion,
new knowledge, systems and formulas. Perceiving their con-
sternation, Jesus decided to teach them how to minister
(beginning in verse 14, I paraphrase):

And He said to His disciples, 'Have them recline to
eat in groups of about fifty each.'

Imagine the disciples issuing those instructions to the crowd. Have you thought those people could not talk? Think what they must have muttered back when they were told, after going all day without a bite to eat, to sit down in groups of fifty.

"What are we going to do?" some asked.

"Don't ask questions; just sit down in groups of fifty."

"What are we going to eat?"

"Well, some fish and bread."

"Where is it? I don't see any catering trucks."

"Uh…I don't want to discuss it; just sit down in groups of fifty."

Can you imagine the fear and trepidation in the hearts of those disciples as they started to carry out the Lord's instructions? When the people were seated, Jesus prayed and blessed it. Many teach that after Jesus prayed, the food started multiplying in His hands. I don't think that was what happened. Actually, He gave it to the disciples, and it multiplied in their hands as they gave it out. Would you have felt a little shaky going to feed your fifty after the Lord had given you only a tail of one fish and a pinch of one edge of bread? But when the first man takes a crumb of bread and a flake of fish, suddenly there is more. And when his wife takes some, there is more and when the next takes some there is more.

Most of us want to say: "Lord, give me a barrel full, and then I won't have any problem believing I can feed them. Let me feel the power resting on my shoulders. Let me feel a warm glow running through my being, then I will go and minister to the world." But the Lord said: "You have a little tail of fish and a little pinch of bread. Go out and get started."

"What if you don't show up?" we say. "I have people out there starving, and they will stone me if I fail them."

But then He says: "I'll go with you to the end of the ages if you'll go out and say My Word. I'll work with you in signs, wonders and authority."

Jesus showed them how to minister in power with feeding the five thousand. When they were through, they had twelve baskets full of scraps. There is a surplus when you do it God's way.

After the feeding of the five thousand, we see the following scenario:

> And it came about that while He was praying alone, the disciples were with Him, and He questioned them, saying, 'Who do the multitudes say that I am?' And they answered and said, 'John the Baptist; but others say Elijah; and others that one of the prophets of old has risen again.' And Peter answered and said, 'The Christ of God.' [The Matthew account has Peter saying: "You are the Christ, the Son of the Living God."] (verses 18-20)

Jesus responds by saying: "Blessed are you, Simon of John, for flesh and blood did not reveal that to you but my Father which is in heaven."

With this Jesus was saying of Peter: "You not only have the power and authority and the ability to preach the kingdom of God and you not only have had a lesson of demonstration by Jesus Himself in how to feed multitudes, but now, Peter, you also have another very important element. You have revelation knowledge. You have exhibited the characteristic that reveals that you know how to move into the holy of holies and hear God for yourself. You don't have to go to some teacher to find out every detail. You have heard God. No man has told you. You didn't arrive at that conclusion on the basis of rational deduction. You didn't get it from inductive Bible study. You got it by revelation. You have heard God for yourself."

This is an essential capacity if we are going to walk with God. To minister, we have to hear God. How did Jesus perform the miracle of the feeding of the multitude? In John, chapter 5, He tells us. He looked into heaven to see what the Father was doing. He found that the Father had a bakery full of bread and a restaurant full of fish. Because he could hear God, He didn't have any problem telling the disciples to seat them in fifties and prepare to feed them before He could see with His eyes that there was plenty of food. To operate in faith we must hear God. How does God express Himself to us? One of the ways when we are a group, particularly when we are ministering to each other, is by giving some member of the group a word of knowledge or a word of wisdom or of faith. That is how the cosmic reality of God breaks in on the physical reality of where we live. But we have to be open to know things that otherwise we could not know.

Sometimes this is an impression in our heart. We just know something. It is like knowing something intuitively. Sometimes you hear something or you see something with your spirit's eye.

I think God comes down to our level on those things. The only way we will accept His communications many times is through the physical realm. But you still must be able to hear God to operate in the supernatural. You cannot go forth blankly and do everything. For one reason the timing is always important. God has the ability to save everyone but have you noticed that everyone does not get saved at once? He has the ability to heal everyone, but have you noticed that everyone does not get healed every time we pray? Why? Because God has a timetable. Sometimes He is using a delay in the situation for His glory, and the timing must be right.

Remember the man in John 9 who was blind from birth? They posed a great theological question for Jesus, asking, "We want to know whether this man is blind because his parents sinned or because he sinned?" Jesus said: "Neither. He is blind so the glory of God can be manifested in him." We do not know how old that man was, but let us say he was twenty-one. For that long he had not received healing. But in God's timing he was healed. The timing was important.

The man of the Gate Beautiful had been lame for many years. He was normally put at the Gate Beautiful by his parents. In the three years of His ministry, Jesus probably walked by this man. But Jesus never did say, "Rise and walk," until one day He walked by in Peter and John. When He walked by in Peter and John, He said, "Now it is time, Rise and walk." That is why you have to hear God.

How do you hear God? Out of *intimate fellowship* with the Father comes revelation from the Father.

Now we see the disciples with authority, power, the ability to preach the kingdom of God with effectiveness, a visible illustration of how to feed multitudes supernaturally and even the ability to hear God personally through revelation knowledge. You may say, "Give me that and I'll make it." But notice what a mess the disciples made with all that equipment.

> But He warned them and instructed them not to tell this to anyone, saying, 'The Son of Man must suffer many things, and be rejected by the elders and chief priests and scribes, and be killed, and be raised up on the third day.' And He was saying to them all, 'If anyone wishes to come after Me, let him deny himself, and take up his cross daily, and follow Me.' (verses 21-23)

Look now at verses 28-33:

> And some eight days after these sayings, it came about that He took along Peter and John and James, and went up to the mountain to pray. And while He was praying, the appearance of His face became different, and His clothing became white and gleaming. And behold, two men were talking with him; and they were Moses and Elijah, who, appearing in glory, were speaking of His departure which he was to accomplish at Jerusalem. Now Peter and his companions had been overcome with sleep; but when they were fully awake, they saw His glory and the two men standing with Him. And it came about, as these were parting from Him, Peter said to Jesus, 'Master, it is good for us to be here; and let us make three tabernacles; one for You, and one for Moses, and one for Elijah' not realizing what he was saying.

Here is Peter, who had power over all the demons and authority over all kinds of sickness; he was able to preach the gospel with effectiveness; he had seen a demonstration of how to feed multitudes supernaturally; he had received revelation knowledge, and yet something was missing. In the midst of glory, Peter became a hero worshipper. The glory of God encompassed Jesus, Moses and Elijah and suddenly Peter talked about building a tabernacle for the three because he was caught up in personalities again. He had seen the greatness of Elijah and Moses and he was trying to put Jesus on the same platform with them. This is a natural tendency for a man who is not controlled by love. Hero worship is one of the worst problems we have today both in the world and in the worldly Church. We will take an athlete, for instance, and because he can swing a baseball bat, we make him an authority on everything from theology to science. He can barely say his name, but he can hit them all over the fence, so the Church says, "We need him on God's side." We do it in a more spiritual way in the Church.

Because we are on television on a daily basis in the Dallas/Fort Worth area, I often get calls from people saying, "You've got to pray for me."

"Well," I say, "I don't mind praying for you, but why don't you call your pastor and get him to pray for you?"

"No. You pray for me."

"Well, don't you have a husband?"

"Yes."

"Get him to pray for you."

"No. You've got to pray for me."

"Do you have any neighbors who are Christians?"

"Yes."

"Get them to pray for you."

"No, You've got to do it."

Now I like to pray for people, but I am no hero or super-star. If you are locked in for one person to pray for you, and you think you can receive from God through only one per-son, you have missed the whole point of being a Christian. A little child may have enough authority and power flowing through him to heal you, and if you are willing for the Lord to touch you through any individual with whom Jesus lives, you might just touch Jesus. That is why it is so important not to cut off other members of the Body. The one you cut off may be the one God intends to use to bless you. You would do well not to stick labels on people, saying, "I'm not as-sociating with them because they have the wrong label." You may need them one day. Some of us are so proud that when we get in trouble emotionally or mentally we would rather call a psychiatrist than a Pentecostal. Some Pentecostals would rather call a psychiatrist than a Baptist. So we go on in our defeat because we will only receive from certain individuals. That is a spiritual manifestation of hero worship. We are doing the same thing that Peter did.

Peter placed Jesus on the same plane as the two men who appeared with Him. In trying to elevate them, he put them on the same level as Jesus. You don't build a tabernacle for Jesus on the same plane with anybody. He doesn't fit there.

I cannot get upset with Peter because I've been impressed with Moses and Elijah, too. I've wanted to get their autograph in the front of my Bible. But that is what is wrong with many of us: hero worship. When we have men on the brain and we think only certain men can do things, we are not controlled by the love of God. The love of God compels you, and you see Jesus in everybody. That is why I ask people to lay hands on one another. Do you know what is happening when you ask somebody else to pray for you? You are saying: "I acknowledge that Jesus is in you; I submit to the Jesus in you. I receive from the Jesus in you, and I want in me the Jesus that is in you."

When the love of God is controlling you, you are absolutely open to your brother, and Jesus is preeminent. Nobody rises up to the same plane with Him.

As we move on to the next account, we see another example of how the disciples handled their resources. Beginning with verse 37:

> And it came about on the next day, that when they had come down from the mountain, a great multitude met Him. And behold, a man from the multitude shouted out, saying, 'Teacher, I beg You to look at my son, for he is my only boy and behold, a spirit seizes him, and he suddenly screams, and it throws him into a convulsion with foaming at the mouth, and as it mauls him, it scarcely leaves him. And I begged Your disciples to cast it out, and they could not.' And Jesus answered and said, 'O unbelieving and perverted generation, how long shall I be with you, and put up with you? Bring your son here.' And while he was still approaching, the demon dashed him to the ground, and threw him into a violent convulsion. But Jesus rebuked the unclean spirit...

Notice that He didn't discuss theology with him; He rebuked him. The word rebuke means "Stop! Cease!" It is the word with which He rebuked the wind when He was in the boat with the disciples. He rebuked the cause of the problem, healed the symptoms of the problem, and restored the relationship of the boy and his father. That is the way Jesus works. When the source is demonic, He deals with the source, clears up the symptoms and then restores the relationship.

This was a strange situation. Didn't we hear Jesus say to those disciples, "You have authority and power over all demons," yet here is a boy who has a demon who is throwing him into convulsions, and these disciples cannot cast him out, even though they outnumber the demon nine to one. Why can't they cast him out? What happened to all their power and authority, revelation knowledge, and faith and to their ability to preach the kingdom of God?

Well, faith only operates through love. Something happened to their love. How do I know? If you want to know what is going on in their hearts, look at what comes out of their mouths a few verses later.

In verse 46, we read: "But an argument arose among them as to which of them might be the greatest." If they were arguing about this in verse 46, they were probably thinking about it in verse 40. It was in their heart. We can safely surmise that they were not controlled by unselfish, undying, unqualified, unconditional love when they were trying to cast out the demon. They were wondering who was going to be the greatest. They were thinking: "We have power, authority, revelation knowledge, and we can go out and perform the kingdom of God and do the works of Jesus. I wonder which of us is the greatest. I have cast out twenty-three demons. How many did you get, James? I was praying with somebody the other night and we saw their leg lengthened; another's cancer was healed. Have you had any major miracles like that? We know it is all of the Lord, but which one of us is the most useful?"

In that kind of attitude, faith stops working because faith works through love. Anything that is stopping the love will stop the faith.

How much authority do you have? How much power do you have? How much revelation knowledge do you have? It means nothing apart from love. Faith works through love. So they were unable to cast out the boy's demon.

Jesus said in another account that it was the kind that comes out by prayer and fasting. I am not sure that the demons are impressed by our prayers and fasting, but I can tell you what happens when you pray and fast. Your soul gets clean, your selfishness is revealed, and you can deal with it so that your faith is freed to move on the track of love. Fasting affects your faith and love more than it does the demons. Then your faith releases your power and your authority. The Lord seems to change the subject in verse 43-44:

> But while everyone was marveling at all that He was doing, He said to His disciples, 'Let these words sink into your eyes; for the Son of Man is going to be delivered into the hands of men.'

Consider that verse carefully. Does it seem complicated to you? "Let these words sink into your ears." Listen to this statement: "For the Son of Man [that's Jesus; He used that term frequently, so it was not a new phrase to the disciples] is going to be delivered into the hands of men." He had said something about that earlier in verse 22: "The Son of Man must suffer many things, and be rejected by the elders and chief priests and scribes, and be killed, and be raised up on the third day." That sounds very straightforward. One should understand what He is talking about. But look at the disciples in verse 45: "But they did not understand this statement, and it was concealed from them, so that they might not perceive it; and they were afraid to ask Him about this statement."

When you have a lack of love — or let's call it what it really is: selfishness — you are not focused on others, as Jesus is, but you are focused on yourself. Such a refusal to focus on others with the love of Jesus is selfishness, and selfishness will block your hearing of the Word of God. It doesn't matter how eloquent a speaker is, if there is selfishness in your heart, you won't hear God speaking. If you do hear the words, you will misunderstand them.

That is why many people today cannot hear God. They may hear the same preachers, listen to the same tapes, read the same books and yet not hear what others can because of selfishness. Self-centeredness keep us from hearing the Lord.

There is a progression revealed in the verses just quoted. Selfishness causes blindness, which causes fear, which often causes pride to arise in reaction. Those who are selfish cannot hear; because they cannot hear, they become scared, which often causes them to put up the false front of pride and prevents their asking the needed questions. Even the Lord's own disciples, His best friends on the earth who walked with Him all the time, fell into this trap. He made a statement and they were afraid to ask Him what He meant.

Why were they afraid to ask Him? They were afraid that He meant what He said. I have a feeling that a lot of people are afraid to ask the Lord what He said because He might say, "I meant exactly what I said." For example, He says, "According to your faith so be it unto you." You hear that and ask: "Lord, what did You mean?" He answers: "I mean, according to your faith, so be it unto you." You say: "Now wait at minute, Lord; that will not work because I've seen people who had all the faith in the world ask for things and they did not get them." But Jesus says, "According to your faith so be it unto you." Again you say, "Lord, if you preach that you will put people under condemnation, because if they don't get it then they feel it was because they didn't have enough faith." So we are afraid to ask the Lord to explain because we are afraid to live with what He says. We reinterpret the Scripture in light of our own selfishness, fear or pride.

What did Jesus mean by "According to your faith so be it unto you?" What confuses some people is their definition of "faith." If you think faith originates in man, you have a problem with the statement. If you realize that faith originates in God, you don't have a problem. "Faithful is He who calls you, and He also will bring it to pass" (I Thessalonians 5:24). We are afraid of finding out what Jesus means because we have already interpreted the scriptures and know what it means in the way we want to understand it. We don't want to ask Jesus because He might want to change our interpretation. But we must start asking the Lord to give us understanding if we are going to believe and live accurately.

The narrative in Luke 9 continues in verse 49:

And John answered and said, 'Master, we saw someone casting out demons in Your name; and we tried to hinder him because he does not follow along with us.'

That is a good thing to do, isn't it? If you cannot cast out demons, don't let anybody else do it. John had been unable to cast one out of the boy in verse 40, but he saw someone else doing it. This man was getting the job done in Jesus' name, but he wasn't wearing the right label. John said, "We told him to stop because he wasn't with us."

Listen to love's answer in verse 50: "Do not hinder him; for he who is not against you is for you." Few of us could ever be that simple, could we? We say: "Now wait, Lord, before we endorse that man we have to know what he believes, who baptized him, who laid hands on him, where he got his ordination papers. We have to understand all that because we cannot afford to endorse everyone." To Jesus it was simple. "If he's not against you, he is for you."

That's love's answer. Knowledge puffeth up, but love is long-suffering. The divisiveness and sectarianism that besets the Church is a result of a lack of love. Denominationalism —not denominations, but denominationalism, the self-seeking devotion to a denomination and the division of the church — is satanic. It is an artificial barrier placed by men to divide Christians whom God told to walk in love with one another and in unity with the Spirit. Verse 51 continues:

> And it came about, when the days were approaching for His ascension, that He resolutely set His face to go to Jerusalem; and He sent messengers on ahead of Him, And they went, and entered a village of the Samaritans, to make arrangements for Him. And they did not receive Him, because He was journeying with His face toward Jerusalem.

When you set your face to go with Jesus, there will be some who will not receive you. They receive you now because your face is set in other directions. But if you set your face to go with Jesus, to do the works of Jesus, whatever the cost, some won't receive you.

How are you going to respond to them? In verse 54, we see how these disciples responded to them. When James and John saw people not receiving Jesus, they said: "Lord do you want us to command fire to come down from heaven and consume them?" They had found a good use for their authority and power. They would make charcoal briquettes out of the Samaritans.

But notice what love says in verse 55: "But He turned and rebuked them and said, 'You don't know what kind of spirit you are of.'" I know what kind of spirit they were of — they were of a destructive spirit. That spirit operates in a lot of disciples. In fact, it operates in every disciple that is not controlled by love. The Son of Man did not come to destroy men's lives but to save them. We have not been given authority to hurt men but to fight the devil and save men: but our tendency is to want to call down fire.

The impression is given that the disciples have power, authority, revelation knowledge, faith and the ability to preach the kingdom of God and yet are still not totally equipped. They will not be equipped until they are baptized in love. They need the baptism and the anointing of the Holy Spirit — that encounter with the Lord that brings an awareness that He actually has told you to feed the five thousand when you have only five pieces of bread and two fish. Then you realize your inadequate resources and say, "Lord, if I'm to be your minister and do the works of Jesus, I must have more than I have now." It is at that moment that you appropriate the Holy Spirit whom you already have living in you, receiving the power for ministry of the Holy Spirit and release of all the gifts of the Holy Spirit within you.

Charles Finney, in explaining an experience much like this, said the Holy Spirit came upon him and empowered him for ministry. After that experience, he had so much power upon his life that many times he would walk through a factory, not saying a word, and people would fall out behind him on the floor in repentance, crying out to God because of the aura of the Spirit of God on him. Sometimes he would go somewhere to preach and, before he would stand in the pulpit, a wave of the Spirit of God would move through the congregation, and people would fall out on the floor.

Incidentally, do not be upset when people start falling out under the power of God. They have been doing that from the beginning. Some groups call it "being slain in the Spirit." But don't let that terminology upset you when God is doing a work. It is reported that during Whitfield and Wesley's day, the power of God would come in such a great surge that people would be knocked out. Thousands of people would come and sit on a hillside to hear Whitfield, and he would say, "You all get down out of those trees. When the power of God comes in a few minutes, you are going to fall, and it will hurt you." Sure enough, when the power of God came, they began falling like cordwood.

We have watched some people merchandise that and exploit it, and some say, "That's not Biblical." But the power of God is always Biblical. During the great awakening people would come under the power of God and begin to quake and shake. They called them the "quakers." Others did something different from quaking. I don't know the difference in quaking and shaking, but they became the group called the Shakers.

I trust that the Lord would come in that kind of power now if He could trust us with His power. When the Lord's power comes, there are many different kinds of physical manifestations because while God doesn't major in the physical, He does not avoid it.

It used to trouble me that when the power of God would come I would start laughing. The devil would say, "You are irreverent." I went along with that condemnation until I was with Miss Bertha Smith, the great Baptist missionary to China. We were experiencing an unusual power of God, and she started laughing. Then I said, "Well, either both of us are irreverent or it's all right."

In other days, I have noticed that in the presence of the power of God I began to tremble. I have heard others say they feel warm. The power of God does affect your physical body, your autonomic nervous system, and it affects different people in different ways.

I was praying for a lady not long ago and, as I held her hand and looked at her, the power of God came on her and her eyelids began to move up and down. That was the only physical manifestation I could see. I held her up, because she was only half conscious for five minutes. God did wonderful things to her while she was caught up in His power, but she didn't shake or quake. Only her eyelids moved. Sometimes you cannot see or feel anything when the power of God comes. Don't be afraid of it either way. He will do His work.

However, that kind of power and authority only runs in the track of love. Would you like to see that kind of power released through you? Returning to the experience Charles Finney had, he described it like this: "It was as though liquid waves of love were flowing through my being." I thought that was an interesting description of what many would call the baptism or the anointing of the Holy Spirit. Whatever experience you have, unless it ultimately issues forth in power manifested through love, you did not get it from God. What He does, He does through love.

Among men and women today on whom I see the power of God rushing and working, I see one common characteristic: they are absolutely in love with Jesus and that love is being released toward men. The power seems to intensify as the love intensifies.

It is interesting to see what Paul calls the baptism or the anointing of the Holy Spirit. Hear what he says in Romans 5:5: "And hope does not disappoint, because the love of God has been poured out within our hearts through the Holy Spirit who was given to us." When was the Holy Spirit given to you? At conversion, when you were saved you received the Holy Spirit, and you received love. So there is a sense in which we can say that what we really need along with the baptism of power is the baptism of love.

How do we get it? We have to receive it. I don't know of anyone who has enough money to buy it. And since it has already been poured out in our hearts, if we have the Holy Spirit, we already have love in us. So we do the same thing with love that you do with the power of the Holy Spirit. We already have the Holy Spirit living within us, but there comes that time when we realize that we are not experiencing love. We are not releasing it. We have it all bound up within us. We only love those who are nice to us. We only love those who have the right label. There comes a time when you must release that love within you and receive the outpouring and the release of the love. You may call it a baptism of love if you like. You don't even have to label it. Just ask and believe.

In preparation for a Bible conference I spent several days in a prayer retreat with several other speakers, and I became aware that in my own heart there had been blockage in love. It broke in my heart. God showed me that one of the reasons that the power of the Spirit was not flowing freely through me was that I had a blockage in love.

After much prayer on my own, I went to a friend and said: "I'd like to ask you and these other men here to lay your hands on me and pray and ask God to give me a real God-given burden for people. I want to love them like Jesus loved them." I will never forget his response. Beginning to cry, he looked at me and said: "I'll do that, but I want you to understand what you're getting into. I want you to understand how it is to start into a city, look at it and no longer see buildings and freeways, but thousands upon thousands of hurting, dying, and sick people. I want you to know how it is to have to spend the first two or three days in that city not being able to sleep for having God impress them on your heart. I want you to know what it is to walk into a restaurant and not be able to enjoy your food because you're seeing people around you as hurting people for whom Jesus died, and you are having to share the gospel with them or get on your knees and pray for them."

It is not a light thing to love as Jesus loves. To love as Jesus loves doesn't just mean that God is going to help you get along with your mother-in-law better. It doesn't just mean that God is going to help you handle that irritating situation at work. It means that you start seeing everybody as Jesus sees them. And when that happens, you have a heavy heart. You have joy and peace but you have a heavy, heavy heart.

Only when you are willing to receive the love can you exercise the power and the authority. One of the ways God shows you His timing is by focusing His love on someone. Have you ever walked into a group of people and suddenly seen one person whom God focused His love on and you just loved that person? It is as though God locks you in on them. You are interested in their need and almost willing to lay down your life for their problem. That is one of the ways God has of saying, "I am ready to work in that person's life." Faith and power will run on that track of love, and when God focuses His love on someone through you, He is usually wanting you to minister to them, and He will release His power in their behalf. That does not mean that He doesn't love everyone else present; it just means it is His timing for you in that particular case.

Would you be willing to open your heart to that kind of love and say: "I want to hurt everywhere Jesus hurts and I want to love everywhere He loves. I'm willing for my body, my mind, my total being to be an instrument not only of the power and authority of Jesus, but of the love of Jesus. Wherever He loves, I will love and minister there"? Would you be willing to do that? That is the missing item in the disciples' equipment until Pentecost. At Pentecost, they received a baptism of power, but that baptism of power was also a baptism of love.

. . . .

Chapter Eight

Ministering The Word

One issue that Christians need to learn during these last days is that it is needless to acquire truth unless you are going to exercise it. If you are a hearer and not a doer, you are deceiving yourself. A major spiritual problem — even among the best of Christians — is deception, because we are continually hearing the Word but not doing it. This is certainly not intentional, but in many churches there is an underlying attitude that by learning just a little more you can be more spiritual. We often judge spiritual maturity by how much we *know*, but God judges by how much we *love*.

Many Christians carry notebooks big enough to give them backaches. Even with all the outlines, precepts, principles and designs they have, their life is still not a ministry. We should be sick and tired of going to church and instead, get ready to *be* the Church. This is not a word just for the church staff — many of us have formed the habit of letting them do the work of the ministry while we just sit and hear the truths. It is time, if we are going to move where God is going, for every Christian to be willing to be a disciple and to perform his part in the ministry. We still have the idea that we have to wait until we know enough before we can do it, but strangely, new Christians are by far the ones who win the most people to the Lord. That is a shame, and it needs to change.

We are called to minister the Word; we must learn how to do this, and what happens when we do minister it.

In Acts 19, we see an illustration of ministering the Word. An unusual little phrase appears in verse 20: "So the Word of the Lord was growing mightily and prevailing." Where the Word of the Lord prevails, things happen. I want you to see what the things are that happen in an atmosphere where the Word is prevailing, as well as how to minister the Word so that is does prevail. Let's just read in Acts 19, beginning with verse 1.

> And it came about that while Apollos was at Corinth, Paul having passed through the upper country came to Ephesus, and found some disciples, and he said to them, 'Did you receive the Holy Spirit when you believed?' And they said to him, 'No, we have not even heard whether there is a Holy Spirit.' And he said, 'Into what then were you baptized?' And they said, 'Into John's baptism.' And Paul said, 'John baptized with the baptism of repentance, telling the people to believe in Him who was coming after him, that is, in Jesus.' And when they heard this, they were baptized in the name of the Lord Jesus. And when Paul had laid his hands upon them, the Holy Spirit came on them, and they began speaking with tongues and prophesying. And there were in all about twelve men.

The main point of that passage is this: These people were so open to truth that when they heard it they received it. Because they received what they heard, they were always getting more. One of the reasons some Christians are locked into their knowledge syndromes is that they have received some truth but are unwilling to turn it loose in order to get more. If the people in this passage had been like many today, they would have said: "John came through, and his preaching was good, and we got it fixed into our system so we don't want to hear anything new. We are John's disciples, and we are sticking to what we know. If your teaching does not fit into what we already have, we are not interested." And they would have missed Jesus. But because they were willing to obey the truth they had, they were getting more revelation. And they did hear more and found new experiences.

Some people today would say: "Well, my experience will do for me. I was baptized in the Jordan River, and that's enough for me. Don't tell me anything about any Holy Spirit." But it is a good idea to go on with the Lord to further revelation. Notice the ministry of the Word in verses 8-10.

> And He entered the synagogue and continued speaking out boldly for three months, reasoning and persuading them about the kingdom of God. But when some were becoming hardened and disobedient, speaking evil of the Way before the multitude, He withdrew from them and took away the disciples, reasoning daily in the school of Tyrannus. And this took place for two years, so that all who lived in Asia heard the word of the Lord, both Jews and Greeks.

It does take time for the Word of God to take root and come up. There has to be a sowing, a watering and a reaping. We want things to happen instantly. We like to get up one morning, have God tell us a truth, then go to church and require everybody there to know what we know. But the *continual* sowing of the Word of God is required if there is to be reaping. One of the reasons we don't see more of the miraculous happenings, such as healing or deliverance or miracles, is that we have not sown that Word.

During our seminars, many people have told me, "I have never heard what you preached." It's from the Bible. The truths have been there a long time. But you cannot expect a crop to come up if the seed has not been sown.

If you want to see something happen in your church or in the people you are ministering to, keep sowing the Word. And when you share the Word, *just* share the Word. Don't share all the reasons it might not work. You may say, "Well, I don't want to lead them astray." They are *already* astray. Give them some truth, and give them a chance to come back.

Don't give answers to people's questions while leaving them in their problems. We spend a great deal of time trying to answer offended hearts. People who are offended have questions. But a person with an offended heart does not want answers — He only wants to use his questions to make accusations. Don't spend your time answering people with an offended heart. Deal with their problem. For example, some say: "What bothers me about preaching on the healing ministry of Jesus is that it puts so many people under condemnation. You tell them they can be healed, and if they believe but don't get healed, they get condemned."

Where does condemnation come from? There is now no condemnation for those who are in Christ Jesus (Romans 8:1). So it definitely does not come from Jesus. What then does it say about a person who is under condemnation? Who is he listening to? He has a hotline to hell. The devil is putting lies right into his mind and he is receiving them.

I agree we should not give fodder to the devil to use in putting condemnation on people, but what is the answer? Should we prevent people from having condemnation by preventing them from having the opportunity to believe? That is just about the only way you can stop all condemnation — by not giving them anything so that they will not misunderstand anything. Just as Peter said concerning Paul's teachings:

> Paul, according to the wisdom given him, wrote as also in all his letters, speaking in them of these things, in which are some things hard to understand, which the untaught and unstable distort, *as they do the rest of the Scriptures to their own destruction.* (II Peter 3:15-16)

The unstable are going to distort almost any teaching, even the Scriptures themselves, so we cannot allow them to dictate what we teach.

In Ephesus Paul did not worry about how people might distort what he said. He spent three months sharing the Word with everybody, and it took three months to divide the group. When you start sharing the Word, it will divide. For three months Paul was sharing and persuading them about the kingdom of God, and then a group of them decided they did not want to go along with those truths. So they caused a big split.

This contradicts the misconception that anything that splits up churches is of the devil. Let me show you how inconsistent we are. Dr. Billy Graham once stated he believed that seventy-five percent of all church members in America were unconverted! Dr. George Truitt, who was a previous pastor of First Baptist Church of Dallas, is reported to have said that he could sleep much better and die with peace if he really believed that fifty percent of his own church members were saved! So it seems that we have a lot of lost people in the Church who are religious. They have been baptized and they believe in their head, but they are going to miss heaven, as someone has said, by about 12 inches — the distance between the heart and the head. When someone comes to a church preaching the unadulterated truth and light of Jesus, the lost people cannot understand, and the church splits. That is normal. Light always splits darkness. But we have a tendency to say: "That's not of God, because God doesn't divide."

Jesus said, "I didn't come to bring peace but a sword." Truth will divide. You are not to be the divider; you are not to judge, saying, "You can go, you can stay." God will divide.

The Word divided the town in Acts 19, and those who were against it were very aggressive in their opposition. So Paul took a group and went to the school of Tyrannus, and for two more years they sowed the Word. Now look what happened when the Word started coming up (verse 11): "And God was performing extraordinary miracles by the hands of Paul."

That word "extraordinary" is worth noting. What happened was so unusual that it was not described as "miracles" but "extraordinary miracles." Some ordinary ones must have been happening too, and I would often be tempted to settle for some of those. But they had some *extraordinary* ones. The power of God was so evident that they were taking pieces of clothing from the preacher's body and sending them to the sick, and people were healed because the power of God was on the clothing.

Many have tried that since without the same results — it is not the method; it is the anointing. I listened to a radio program when I was in seminary that offered to send out prayer cloths, and I laughed about that. Now I don't know if they were right or wrong, but I do know this: nobody was asking for any of my clothing, because mine didn't have any power on it! The best they could have gotten out of mine was perspiration. But when the Word of God is sown, and it is sown purely and watered properly, it will come up and it will sometimes come up in the form of extraordinary miracles. Until the extraordinary ones get here, though, let's be happy enjoying the ordinary ones — and let's not be satisfied until we see them.

The story continues in Acts 19:12:

> So that handkerchiefs or aprons were even carried from his body to the sick, and the diseases left them and the evil spirits went out. But also some of the Jewish exorcists, who went from place to place, attempted to name over those who had the evil spirits the name of the Lord Jesus, saying, 'I adjure you be Jesus whom Paul preaches' And seven sons of one

Sceva, a Jewish chief priest, were doing this. And the evil spirit answered and said to them, 'I recognize Jesus, and I know about Paul, but who are you?' And the man, in whom was the evil spirit, leaped on them and subdued both of them and overpowered them, so that they fled out of that house naked and wounded. And this became known to all, both Jews and Greeks, who lived in Ephesus; and fear fell upon them all and the name of the Lord Jesus was being magnified.

When we start seeing the real power of the word of God producing the same thing that it produced through Paul, there will be just as many imitators who create problems as there will be persecutors. We cannot let the imitators alarm us — it should even be considered an encouraging sign. How long has it been since anyone wanted to imitate us? Who do you know that uses the name of Jesus well enough that anybody wants to copy them? There will be those like the Jewish exorcists who said: "Hey, that dude has power. He doesn't have to do incantations or anything; he just says, 'in the name of Jesus,' and the demons flee. Let's try that." But God was even glorified in their folly.

We must not let the fear of abuse keep us from taking what God wants to give us. There is a proverb that says: "Where there are no oxen, the stall is clean." We have a lot of clean stalls. They call them churches. There is no mess because there are no oxen, and likewise there is no increase that comes from the strength of the oxen. We know exactly what is going to happen from the moment we walk in until the moment we leave. There will be no strange happenings. Nothing will make us feel uncomfortable. Nobody is going to do anything extraordinary. Nobody will get out of the ordinary. We are all going to breathe at the same time. We are all going to kneel at the same time. We are all going to give at the same time. We will sing at the same time, with the same intonation. We will do everything as we have always done it so there won't be any mess. You can feel comfortable bringing anybody here, because we have a clean stall *and no oxen.*

Now if you get an ox, he may mess up the stall. But you also have something that will work, right? Would you be willing to clean up the stall once in a while if the glory of God comes in the Word?

Just say the Word, exactly as it is, and you will have some people misunderstanding it. There will be some who think they can claim healing any time they wish and the result will be a big mess. But when that happens, just sit down and love them and tell them the truth. We may have people stand up and speak out of order. If somebody does that, don't get uptight. If it is abused, gently correct it. If you listen, you might get blessed.

Aren't you glad that God has been lenient and patient with you in cleaning up the messes you have made? Then don't you think we should help each other? Do you think God would let something happen that He couldn't handle? Let's remember that it is *His* Church.

A mess developed where Paul was preaching, but the Lord took care of it. He even used the demons to help clean it up. He used the demons to correct those who had been trying to copy the miracles. Now notice the results of the mess and the correction of it (verse 17):

> And this became known to all, both Jews and Greeks, who lived in Ephesus; and fear fell upon them all and the name of the Lord Jesus was being magnified.

Isn't that what we want? We are forever saying, "Oh, Lord, magnify your name." The Lord says: "All right, I will tell you how I want to magnify my name. I will let someone copy the power of God, let a demon jump on them, beat them up, tear all their clothes off, and then I am going to correct them on the spot."

What happened next is most important. Some today say they wish we would get away from signs, wonders and miracles and get back to repentance. But the only thing that produces repentance is the unadulterated sowing, watering, and harvesting of the Word of God. We have not seen much repentance in a long time. We have seen a lot of man-manipulated confession, regret, remorse and condemnation, but that is not repentance. We preach behavior modification, beat people over the head with condemnation and hold witnessing, prayer and Spirit-filled living over their heads; and they all say, "Oh, I wish I could live up there but I can't." They get on their knees and they think they are repenting but many are just having a 'pity party.'

When you repent, things change. Let the Word show you some genuine repentance in a place where the Word of God is prevailing.

> Many also of those who had believed kept coming, confessing and disclosing their practices. (verse 18)

We know we have little repentance today because business practices don't change, home practices don't change, personal and private practices don't change. But what happened in Ephesus (verse 19)?

> And many of those who practiced magic brought their books together and began burning them in the sight of all; and they counted up the price of them and found it fifty thousand pieces of silver [today's equivalent would be two million dollars].

They burned two million dollars worth of art work, magic and books. That is serious repentance. We can't seem to get serious enough to repent today — to sell a car, to give up a habit or to sell a house. I am sure in the incident at hand that some were saying, "Don't burn it, sell it and give the money to the poor." There have always been Judases around. But these people showed serious repenting and that was the result of the Word being sown. The narrative continues: "So the word of the Lord was growing mightily and prevailing" (verse 20).

If we are going to live in an atmosphere of ministering, we must live in an atmosphere in which the Word is prevailing. However, the Word cannot prevail until it is first sown.

In Mark 4, beginning with verse 1, Jesus teaches about sowing:

> And He began to teach again by the seashore. And such a very great multitude gathered before Him that He got into a boat in the sea and sat down; and all the multitude were by the seashore on the land. And He was teaching them many things in parables, and was saying to them in His teaching, 'Listen to this! Behold, the sower went out to sow; and it came about that as he was sowing, some seed fell beside the road, and

the birds came and ate it up. And other seed fell on the rocky ground where it did not have much soil; and immediately it sprang up because it had no depth of soil. And after the sun had risen, it was scorched; and because it had no root, it withered away. And other seed fell among the thorns, and the thorns grew up and choked it, and it yielded no crop. And other seeds fell into the good soil and as they grew up and increased, they yielded a crop and produced thirty, sixty, and a hundredfold.' And He was saying, 'He who has ears to hear, let him hear.' And as soon as He was alone, His followers, along with the twelve, began asking Him about the parables. And He was saying to them, 'To you has been given the mystery of the kingdom of God.'

What a powerful phrase! "To you has been given the mystery of the kingdom of God." We have it all and it is a gift.

But those who are outside get everything in parables, in order that while seeing, they may see and not perceive; and while hearing, they may hear and not understand lest they return and be forgiven.

Does it sound to you as if spiritual truth comes only to those who have ears to hear and that others will hear the words but not the meaning? Yet today we have reduced Biblical interpretation to what the rational mind can deduce and we say that, with proper use of merely rational hermeneutical tools, every man can arrive at a true interpretation of the Scriptures. Pardon me, but there is a hermeneutical word for that: "baloney"!

Verse 13 continues: "And He said to them, 'Do you not understand this parable? And how will you understand all the parables?'"

This parable is a key to all the parables. Spiritual understanding is the key to everything Jesus said. If you don't understand some of the things He says here in this parable, you are going to miss much of the Word of God, because this is a parable about the Word of God, and everything God does He does through a Word. Knowing the importance of the parables, Jesus explains it.

> The sower sows the word, And these are the ones who are beside the road where the word is sown; and when they hear, immediately Satan comes and takes away the word which has been sown in them.

The first thing we need to understand is that Satan immediately attacks every word you sow. We think that because someone hears the Word, they have it. They may have heard a passage many times and think they know it. But when the Word is sown, if you don't immediately receive it, Satan immediately snatches it out of your heart. You can still tell what the verse says, but you can't tell what *Jesus* said. That word doesn't produce fruit in your life.

When the seed falls into good soil, it will bear fruit. What kind of fruit will it bear? The fruit of the Word: the fruit seen in the life of Jesus, the Living Word. The works of Jesus will be done.

If you think you have the truth but are not producing the Word, the works of Jesus, then you have missed it. When you heard the Word in your head, you did not receive it, and the devil snatched it away. The ministry of sowing the Word is spiritual warfare. Every time you sow a seed, it is either going to be received and produce fruit or the devil is going to steal it.

Jesus uses three analogies to depict hindrances to receiving the Word. The hard packed road represents tradition. Some seed fall where people have walked back and forth, packing the soil. It has become so hardened under the travel that it cannot receive the seed. Some people cannot receive the word because the word is sown in their head and their minds are hardened by tradition. Their hearts are closed to new knowledge, so the Word does not produce fruit. Then it is easy for Satan to steal it.

> And in a similar way these are the ones on whom seed was sown on the rocky places, who, when they hear the word, immediately receive it with joy. (verse 16)

We all have rocky places in our lives — times when things are going badly. In those times we want relief, and we will immediately jump on any word we get. But it will not hold because when persecution comes, we fold. A lot of people don't really want to repent; they just want relief. They are grabbing for something to ease a temporary situation in their life. They do not embrace the Word with their hearts. The way to recognize this is to see that when persecution begins, they fall away. If you receive the Word, it produces fruit in you every time. As verse 17 says: "And they have no firm root in themselves, but are only temporary; then, when affliction or persecution arises because of the Word, immediately they fall away."

Then there is another kind of soil.

> And others are the ones on whom seed was sown among the thorns [there are already thorns growing there]. These are the ones who have heard the Word, and the worries of the world, and the deceitfulness of riches, and the desires for other things enter in and choke the Word, and it becomes unfruitful. (verse 18)

In sowing we really have a battle with this soil, because there are very few people who do not have previous programming. They are conditioned to desire the deceitfulness of riches, and all this is choking out the Word.

> And those are the ones on whom seed was sown on the good soil; and they hear the Word and accept it, and bear fruit, thirty, sixty, and a hundredfold. (verse 20)

If you hear the Word and you accept it, you bear fruit. What fruit? The Word performs in you exactly what it says. You do the works of Jesus, who is the Living Word. When the Word has its way in you, you work like Jesus. If that is not happening, you are not receiving the Word.

Since we know that the Word has to be sown before it can sprout, we know we must sow and, as we sow, we must understand why some seeds don't produce. But the good news is that some of it will fall on good soil, and we should focus on the good.

One other word on sowing: You should sow what you want to reap. We have been sowing for years that every church should be an evangelistic church. Basically, we have preached a very simple evangelism. In my personal opinion, we have preached a watered down, perverted concept of evangelism that produces a distorted Christian life; one look at the converts reveals this. We are harvesting just what we have sown.

Jesus went forth preaching the kingdom of God. Do you know what He reaped? He reaped people of the kingdom, people who knew how to live in the kingdom life. In Luke 4:18 he, himself, defines His preaching, and we will see what he reaped.

> 'The Spirit of the Lord is upon Me, because He anointed me to preach the gospel to the poor. [The poor responded, and people were saved.] He has sent me to proclaim release to the captives. [He preached deliverance and people were delivered.] And recovery of sight to the blind, to set free those who are downtrodden, to proclaim the favorable year of the Lord.'

After the planting, there must be watering. Isaiah 55 reveals the watering concept, beginning with verse 1:

> 'Ho! Everyone who thirsts, come to the waters; And you who have no money come, buy and eat. Come, buy wine and milk without money and without cost. Why do you spend money for what is not bread, and your wages for what does not satisfy? Listen carefully to me, and eat what is good, and delight yourself in abundance. Incline your ear and come to me. Listen, that you may live.'

What is the water? His words. It is what He is saying. He is saying,

'Listen that you may live; and I will make an everlasting covenant with you, according to the faithful mercies shown to David.' (verse 3)

'For as the rain and the snow come down from heaven, and do not return there without watering the earth, and making it bear and sprout, and furnishing seed to the sower and bread to the eater; So shall my word be which goes forth from my mouth; it shall not return to me empty, without accomplishing what I desire, and without succeeding in the matter for which I sent it.' (verses 10 & 11)

Isn't that good news? If we will just speak His Word, He said His Word will water the Word we have sown. I sow His Word and I water His Word by proclaiming His Word. He says He will water it and make it come up, and it will not return without accomplishing what He sent it out to do.

We can see the very work of God done if we will stick with the Word. There is sowing and watering, and we must give it a little time to grow. Then comes the harvest. We find that in Mark 4:21:

And He was saying to them, 'A lamp is not brought to be put under a peck-measure, is it, or under a bed? Is it not brought to be put on the lampstand?'

When God tells you something and it is so different from the way everyone around you thinks and behaves, the tendency is to put it in a peck-measure or under a bed. You want to say: "Oh, they won't listen. They wouldn't receive it. It's too new." You feel you need to put limits on it. But Jesus says:

"Don't put any limit on it, and don't put it under a bed where you are only going to rest on it. Put it on a lampstand."

You may say: "But it's going to scare some people." God is responsible. It is *His* Word. Scaring people is a risk you took when you decided to be one of His disciples and when you got into the ministry of the Word. You may speak His Word and when you do, yes, there is going to be some misunderstanding and some persecution.

He said, "I'll watch over my Word and I'll perform it." It's not always going to be successful. You are going to sow some on a rocky road. You are going to sow some in thorny ground. But, you are going to have some fall into good soil. Put it on a lampstand.

James Robison uses a great illustration for this. He says the Lord didn't tell us to turn on a spotlight and shine it in everybody's eyes, to rush up to someone walking in darkness, shine a spotlight into his face and say, "See!" It will hurt his eyes. Put it on a lampstand and just let it shine. It will give light to all who are in the house. And those who don't like the house will get out.

Jesus continues in verse 22:

> For nothing is hidden, except to be revealed; nor has anything been secret, but that it should come to light. If any man has ears to hear, let him hear. And He was saying to them, 'Take care what you listen to. By your standard of measure it shall be measured to you; and more shall be given you besides. For whoever has, to him shall more be given; and whoever does not have, even what he has shall be taken away from him.'

Now notice the harvest principle in verse 26:

> And He was saying, 'The kingdom of God is like a
> man who casts seed upon the soil; and goes to bed at
> night and gets up by day, and the seed sprouts up
> and grows — how, he himself does not know.'

That is one of the great thrills about being the Church. Just say the Word as Jesus does. Some people may get angry and some may get confused, but suddenly you will see the Word beginning to sprout in someone. They will be changing. You will say: "How did that happen?" You won't know how, but it will be happening. It won't be because you poked all of your information into their ears. All you did was lay the Word out, go on to bed and, lo, when you woke up it was growing.

We have seriously misunderstood discipleship. We have thought that we have to take the responsibility to disciple our brother. So we take him to our side and teach him everything we know and train him to think as we do and interpret scripture as we do. We teach him the philosophy and world view that we have. We lead him to approach problems the way we do. Then we think we have made a disciple. We have to meet together many times to accomplish that.

The problem is that one day we have to say, "All right, brother, you've got to leave the nest now and get out there and start doing things." He goes out and runs into a little problem. The first thing he thinks is: "I wonder what my brother would say I should do?" When I make a disciple like that, I have made a disciple of me. To make disciples of Jesus, one of the first things we must do is teach him to hear Jesus.

Plant the Word. Just say the Word and let the Word do its work so he can learn to hear Jesus.

That is a bit risky, because if your brother learns to hear Jesus, he may hear Jesus say something you didn't hear Him say. Which means he will be teaching you, though you are the "discipler," not the "disciple."

If you are going to make disciples of Jesus, you have to teach them to hear Jesus. Then when one faces a problem, he doesn't say, "I wonder what my brother or sister would do?" He says, "Jesus, what are we going to do?" And he and Jesus will move right on through the problem. That is true disciple making.

The only way you can make disciples is by sowing the Word, watering the Word, and letting it come up with that mystery of God. I don't know how it works. I don't know how a grain of corn turns into a stalk of corn. But I know it works. That is what Jesus says: "How [it grows], he himself does not know."

"The soil produces crops by itself" (verse 28). (You don't have to go out and get it to.) You don't plant a seed, then stand there and say, "Oh, please come up, please produce fruit." It just does, first the blade, then the head, then the mature grain in the head.

Please let it mature. When the Word starts growing a little in someone, we see a blade and we want to make them the chairman of every committee in the church. We start harvesting immediately. When he gets a blade, he is just growing. Let him grow! If he forms the head, he is still maturing. Wheat makes the head before the grain develops in it. As you look at it, it appears to be mature, but there is nothing in it. Think of how corn matures. The shuck develops, but all that is inside is the bare cob. It looks fruitful, but if you feel it, you will discover that it is still empty inside. Let it mature, then there will be a harvest. It may be three months. There was such a harvest in Ephesus, where Paul sowed. But when the crop came up, it came up good. They had extraordinary miracles, which people wanted to copy. Then it is time to put in the sickle.

> 'But when the crop permits [the only one who knows exactly when the crop is ready is the Lord Himself] he immediately puts in the sickle because the harvest is come.' (verse 29)

How do you put in the sickle? When the Word has been sown — the unadulterated pure Word of Jesus — when it has been watered with prayer and with love and cultivated by cleaning up the messes, then you speak the Word with authority. That is putting in the sickle.

You stand up with authority and say: "In the name of Jesus, you who are lost and want to be saved, come to Jesus now. He will save you now." You say: "Come. Jesus is here. If you come to Jesus, He will save you today." You say it authoritatively. That is putting in the sickle.

Some men are more gifted than others, but any of us can do it if we find a field that is ready. If you have sown the word of healing, and shared the word of how Jesus is the healer and have shared the healing, a day can come when the Lord will speak to you and say, "It is time." And you can say to them: "Listen, Jesus is the healer, and today if you are sick, you can come and Jesus will meet you here, and you will find healing in Jesus' name."

If you have preached the word of deliverance and sown and watered the seed of deliverance, there will come the day when you can say: "Jesus will set you free. He came to set captives free. If you will come to Him, you can be delivered now."

Many times you will put the word of authority out with a word of knowledge. You will know. That is how you know that the crop is ready. You will be going about His business and the Lord will speak to you. He will say: "I am doing something right now. I am reaping right now. There is someone here right now who is lost and wanting to be saved and I am saving right now." When the Lord tells you that, you stand up and say: "Jesus of Nazareth is saving someone right now. If that someone is you, come forth and let us know about it."

The Lord may say to you: "I am healing tonight. There is power for healing and there are three people here whom I want to heal." When He says that, it is time to put in the sickle. Say: "If it is you whom the Lord wants to heal, if it is in your heart and you want to be healed, come right now and share with us how Jesus is healing you. If you want us to join with you in prayer, we will."

Do you see how to put in the sickle? It may not happen in a formal service. The Lord may awaken you one night and say: "I am saving Brother Sam right now. It is time for him to be saved. I'll save him right now if he will ask me." Call Sam on the phone and say: "Brother Sam, I love you. Just wanted you to know that Jesus is in the saving business, and He would like to save you right now. Could I pray with you that you would be saved?" Then reap the harvest.

The Lord may say: "Mrs. Smith has been under a great burden. She has been hurting badly. Her heart has been broken. She has been laboring under all kinds of problems. I have come to heal her broken heart, set her free and deliver her from all that oppression and affliction. I'm in that business tonight; I'm doing it right now." If God puts that in your heart, it is time to put in the sickle. Go to see her. Reap. You will reap if you faint not. If you sow and water, you will reap.

Living in that manner, you can *be* Church, rather than just going to church. Don't you get tired of just going to church? I think it is amusing that we have retreats in our churches. The only thing we retreat from is going to church. We need that retreat. We go to church so much we get tired. We are weary of going to meetings. What do we do when we go to a retreat? We go to another meeting. We go to meetings to rest up from going to meetings. It is good to go to a retreat, but retreats would be much better if we were out there in life being the church all the time, sowing, watering, fighting the battle, praying over people, sharing with people, loving people and meeting their needs. While you are out there doing these things, sometimes you need to get back with just Christians and retreat to love each other, minister to each other and be restored. That kind of retreat will really help you.

I suspect that one of the reasons many of us are having trouble doing all of these things is that we have not taken the first step. Jesus said to his disciples: "I want you to go into all

Israel and preach the gospel and heal and deliver." Then He added this: "Freely you have received, freely give." He is not asking us to give anything that we have not already received.

Could it be that we are not able to perform the Word because we have not really received it? You cannot give away what you do not have. Are you sure that you received the Word in your own heart? If so, you can be a producer, you can do the works of Jesus. You can release Him, in all authority, power and resources, to do His works through you.

Now the only remaining step is to go out, stop just talking about it and let Him *do* it. When the Lord is present, everything He has is available — His salvation, His redemption, His sanctification, His healing, His deliverance. You can receive anything He has. Please don't miss the great thrill of encountering God in ministry.

What do you need? Your need is on the altar on which you meet God. We have invited Him to come and He has been pleased to come. So, as you sense the presence of God, just receive from Him. If He tells you something to put the sickle to, then do it.

Chapter Nine

Be The Church

As we grow spiritually, we go through certain stages. Each stage has its dangers, but each also has its privileges and we will begin to see these in I John 2:7-17:

> Beloved, I am not writing a new commandment to you, but an old commandment which you have had from the beginning; the old commandment is the word which you have heard. On the other hand, I am writing a new commandment to you, which is true in Him and in you, because the darkness is passing away, and the true light is already shining.

What is He saying? "I'm not giving you a new commandment. You have heard these words before, but I'm giving you a new commandment because it has new meaning with new power." He continues:

> The one who loves his brother abides in the light and there is no cause for stumbling in him. But the one who hates his brother is in the darkness and walks in the darkness, and does not know where he is going because the darkness has blinded his eyes. I am writing to you, little children [about this new commandment, that's not really a new commandment but an old commandment that is new to you because it has

new power in it], because your sins are forgiven you for His Name's sake. I am writing to you, fathers, because you know Him who has been from the beginning. I am writing to you, young men, because you have overcome the evil one. I have written to you, children, because you know the Father. Do not love the world, not the things in the world. If anyone loves the world, the love of the Father is not in him. For all that is in the world, the lust of the flesh and the lust of the eyes and the boastful pride of life, is not from the Father, but is from the world. And the world is passing away, and also its lusts; but the one who does the will of God abides forever.

This passage is full of much beautiful truths, but notice especially the stages of spiritual growth that all must experience and what happens at each of these levels. We need to know the stages, because we have a tendency to want to be at some level other than where we are. We seem to want to skip what we must learn at each level. This is true as we grow up physically. Have you ever known children who wanted to be grown without going through the stages of growing up? No matter what age they are, they are dissatisfied with it, because they are trying to live as if they are older. When they get old, they wish they were young again and try to live in the past. So people either tend to live in the future or in the past. Nobody wants to live in the present. But if you don't live in the present, physically, you will never be prepared to live in the future.

The same is true spiritually. We have set our goal to be spiritually mature and sometimes we get our eyes so fixed on that goal that we don't enjoy the stage we are in at the moment.

The first thing that's important to know as little children is that you are a member of a family. God teaches you to become family conscious in your heart and in your mind. We need to develop spiritual family consciousness.

John said two things about the children. He said, "I am writing to you, children, because your sins are forgiven you for Jesus' sake, and I am writing to you, children, because you know the Father." Basically, then, spiritual children must settle two things: forgiveness and fatherhood.

God wants you to know that you are forgiven for Jesus' sake. The reason many of us cannot progress in spiritual growth is that we have never embraced the truth that we are forgiven for Jesus' sake. We tend to believe we are forgiven on the basis of how long we confess or how remorseful we feel or how much we try to do better, but the fact is we are forgiven on the basis of grace. Some have been critical of the Catholic Church, saying that they have provided a way into the presence of God other than Jesus, that they have said you can come through the confessional and penance. Ironically the Protestants have done the same thing. Ask the average Protestant, if he is not right with God, what he must do to get back into fellowship with Him and he will say, "Confess your sins to get back to God."

You might respond: "I thought you told me there was only one way to God. I thought you were one of those Protestants who believe in grace, who said Jesus is the only way to God. If He is the only way the first time, He is the only way the second and the third time. What do you mean, telling people they can confess back into the presence of God?"

But many evangelical Christians believe that. So they confess and confess, trying to get back to God. The fact is that if you want to get in fellowship with God, you don't have to go anywhere or do anything. You only have to believe something. You have to believe in grace; that is, that the blood of Jesus has already provided the way into the presence of God, and you enter in because your sins are forgiven you for His sake. Your sins are not forgiven on the basis of how long you confess, or where you go or how remorseful and guilty you feel or anything good you do to make up for it. They are forgiven for Jesus' sake. Has Jesus changed? Has His blood lost its power, its efficacy, its effectiveness? It is the blood of Jesus that gives us the right to go into the presence of God. Hebrews 10:14-22 presents a beautiful picture of this truth. Speaking of the intercessory work of Jesus, it says: "For by one offering He has perfected [past tense] for all time those who are sanctified." Who are those who are sanctified? Believers are the sanctified.

> And the Holy Spirit also bears witness to us; for after saying, 'This is the covenant that I will make with them after those days,' says the Lord: 'I will put my laws upon their heart, and upon their mind I will write them.' He then says, 'And their sins and their lawless deeds I will remember no more. Now where there is forgiveness of these things, there is no longer any offering for sin.'

That means that Jesus is not going to make an offering — and that there is no need for you to make one. You do not have to make an offering by promising God you are going to do better or by committing yourself to the ministry and going to the mission field or by feeling guilty. There is no longer any offering for sin. Continuing with verse 19, it says: "Since therefore, brethren, we have confidence to enter the holy place by the blood of Jesus..."

By what? He didn't say by how holy you have been living, by how much you have been praying, by how disciplined you have been. You have a confidence to enter the holy place by the blood of Jesus.

Does that ever change? Of course not. Then there is never any separation between you and God. The sense of separation is an illusion. It is deception that the enemy puts upon you and you receive. There is no separation.

> We have confidence to enter the holy place by the blood of Jesus, by a new and living way which He inaugurated for us through the veil, that is, His flesh, and since we have a great priest over the house of God, let us draw near [that means enter in] with a sincere heart in full assurance of faith, having our hearts sprinkled clean from an evil conscience and our bodies washed with pure water (Hebrews 10:19-22)

This is not to negate the need for repentance when it is timely, but the first thing a Christian needs, as a spiritual child, is an understanding of forgiveness. Repentance is how we see grace but it is not how we get it; we receive grace by the blood of the Lamb. We do not receive God's grace because of the quality of our repentance but by the quality of our Lord's sacrifice. He has already accomplished what needs to be done for our acceptance. True repentance comes *after* we have seen what He has done for us, not in order to see it.

As I deal with people in varied areas of ministry, I find very few people who know what it means to be forgiven. They are living in condemnation, in guilt and under the burden of trying to get good enough to be delivered. You may not have been able to see the glory of God in your life. If not, the reason may be you don't think you are worthy of God's love. God has moved toward you in a soft, gentle, powerful way, wanting to put His arms around you, love you and pour out His blessings on you. He encounters the attitude that "Well, this couldn't be for me because I'm just not worthy of it, I haven't been good enough." If that depicts your life, you have a problem with your own forgiveness. Before you can receive God's blessings for ministry to others, you must receive His forgiveness for yourself. You must be forgiven for Jesus' sake.

The second thing you must know, as a part of this family consciousness, is that God is your Father. There is a "daddy" relationship. I do not mean to seem irreverent, and I am sure there was more reverence in the phrase, "Abba! Father!" that we find in Romans 8:15 than there is in our phrase "daddy." We have made that a very common term, and God is never to be referred to in common terminology. But the Holy Spirit brings the reality of God to you so that you know Him as Father.

There is a current misconception that if you grew up in a home where the father image was not good, or you and your father had a poor relationship, you will have trouble relating to God. That is not necessarily true. It is not your natural inclination and how you learn to love your biological father that enables you to love God anyway. It says that "we have received a spirit of adoption...by which we cry, 'Abba! Father!'" It is not your natural learning but the Spirit of God who gives you the ability to know God as Father. You may never have heard of a father, but when you move into that spirit of adoption, suddenly you know God as Father. If the father image was not good in your home, you can stop letting Satan give you that as a barrier to a "Daddy" relationship with God.

Christians in the children's stage cannot move on to adolescence spiritually until their forgiveness and God's Fatherhood have become real to them. What is your concept of God? Is He still the teacher? A lot of people see God that way. They believe that everything that happens to them is some lesson God is trying to teach them. A good father does teach, but a good father is not just a teacher.

When my little girl was trying to learn to ride her bicycle, I told her not to go up and down the hill beside the house. She thought she could ride better then she really could, so she rode down the hill and fell. She bruised and scratched herself badly. What should I do as a father? Run out to her while she is bleeding all over, sit her on the curb and say: "All right, Karis, what did you learn by this?" No, that is not what a father does. He runs out, picks her up, hugs her, loves her, washes off those wounds and kisses her. He lets her cry on his shoulder, sympathizes with her, and cries a little with her. In time, he may do some teaching, but right then is a time for loving. Do you ever let God love you, or do you just see Him as a teacher?

Some see Him as a king. Kings are always issuing edicts to do this and do that. Those who see God as a king only go to Him when they need a command.

It is all right to sit in God's presence in a family relationship, and that really is where we need to begin in our relationship to Him. Sit on his knee and let Him love you. That is what children need to know. Many have tried to move into adolescence and mature spiritual adulthood who have never learned to relate to God as Father. When they get into the warfare and are trying to fight the enemy, they don't know how to go back to the Father and receive His love and care. They see God only as a commander of the army. When you see God as the Commander of the army, and you see all the other Christians as fellow soldiers, then when one of them gets hit, you just roll him over into a ditch and go on. But when you see every Christian as a brother, you can't find yourself stepping over bodies and rolling them into ditches. You find yourself bent over them, weeping and trying to help them back to health.

Family consciousness is an absolute necessity, and you will never know one another as brothers and sisters until you know God as Father. But neither can you know Him as Father without knowing one another as brothers and sisters. The two work together. When true family consciousness exists, the childhood stage can be enjoyed. If you are in the childhood stage, don't try to pretend you are somewhere else. Enjoy being a kid.

You may be saying, "I don't want anybody saying I am in the children's stage; I've been a Christian twenty years, and it's time for me to be a father." I agree that it is time, but if you're not a father, you're not. Pretending won't help you. Enjoy being a kid until you've learned what God wants to teach you, then you can move on to the next stage.

The next stage is the young man's stage. What did John say about them? He said: "I write to you, young men, because you have overcome the evil one, and I have written to you because you are strong, and the word of God abides in you."

When you move from the childhood stage into the young man's stage, you move from consciousness of family into consciousness of victory. And when you move into consciousness of victory, you are moving away from the comforts of home and your relationship with the Father and your family. You are realizing that you have an enemy and he must be faced. Luke 10:17-20 is a scripture that shows children moving into adolescence. They are moving into the young man's stage. Jesus has sent out seventy disciples, and now they are returning.

> And the seventy returned with joy, saying, 'Lord, even the demons are subject to us in Your name.' And He said to them, 'I was watching Satan fall from heaven like lightning. Behold, I have given you authority to tread upon serpents and scorpions, and over all the power of the enemy, and nothing shall injure you. Nevertheless do not rejoice in this, that the spirits are subject to you, but rejoice that your names are recorded in heaven.'

Jesus is getting them back to understanding the basics. The basics are that your sins are forgiven you for His sake.

> At that very time He rejoiced greatly in the Holy Spirit, and said, 'I praise Thee, O Father, Lord of

heaven and earth, that Thou didst hide these things from the wise and intelligent and didst reveal them to babes. Yes, father, for thus it was well-pleasing in Thy sight.' (verse 21)

Did you hear what He said? Who received that revelation of their victory, strength and power when they were overcoming nations? Babes. Jesus is moving them from the babe stage, the childhood stage, to the victory conscious stage, and He is thrilled about it.

You may have been inching into that realm. The Lord is introducing you into warfare and acquainting you with the fact that there is an enemy to be faced. You may have started fighting the enemy. Among those at this stage, there is a tendency to say: "Well, we're finally mature. We can handle the devil now. We know our victory in Jesus, and that's all there is to life."

No, that is not maturity. You fight the enemy for victory only so you can go on about the business of doing what you were sent into the world to do. After great victories, the conquerors do not quit — their work is really just beginning. After the victory there is occupation and rebuilding. What did the our troops do after we won World War II? We immediately sought to bring the world back to normal. Then many troops returned home and resumed their lives. Well, after spiritual victory, we need to find out what life is all about and resume it. The goal of the war was to get the world back to where normal life could resume.

Notice though what characterizes the young man's stage. "You are strong" — strong in the Lord, in your body and in the Word. If I evaluate correctly what is going on in the Church, God is moving children into the young man's stage; that explains the emphasis on spiritual warfare. Victory is not the stopping point, but it is an important stage we must go through. What is the issue at this stage? Abiding in the Word, being strong in the Word and discovering your overcoming nature. We have had a tendency to believe that who you are in Christ is the epitome of all teaching. I'm confessing who I am in Christ and I'm in the Word and the Word is coming alive to me, and that is all wonderful. But at that point we are just moving into adolescence.

We all have a tendency to camp on the latest revelation we have received and make that the test of fellowship, the essence of all spirituality and the secret to solving all problems. I have done that many times.

I was converted at an early age, and I don't have many memories of that experience. But I can remember that when I was thirteen I went to a youth camp, and the Word of God began to prick my heart and people were using the phrases "the Lordship of Jesus" and "Jesus is Lord." It made spiritual sense. I realized that, although I had trusted Jesus earlier, I knew nothing about His being Lord of my daily walk. When that truth dawned on me, I thought it was the epitome of all truth. It was the solution to all problems. I would say to everyone I saw: "I can tell you what is wrong with you. You just haven't made Jesus Lord. You have Him as Savior, but you don't have Him as Lord." If you shared with me about a family problem, your problem was that Jesus was not Lord. If you had a financial problem, your problem was that Jesus was not Lord.

This is a great truth and God does use it to perform wonderful works in people's lives. When I was in seminary, a fellow visited from Asbury Seminary, where they had experienced a measure of revival. In a chapel program, he spoke only a few words, but then held up three fingers and said, "Jesus is Lord," and sat down. I thought, "Hmmm, I knew that." By then, it was old news to me. But the power of God moved in that place, and people started going to the front of the chapel, praying and confessing sin to one another. Soon the chapel was filled with people praying throughout the day and into the night, and prayer meetings sprang up all over the campus because someone came along and said, "Jesus is Lord," and held up three fingers.

It is a wonderful revelation. The Lord wants us to know it. But there is a tendency to say, "That's it; that's all the truth," and remain stuck at that stage.

At another camp I attended, the emphasis was on the filling of the Spirit. Miss Bertha Smith was there. She opened a new dimension in my life, and I received the filling of the Holy Spirit for the first time, and I said: "That is it. That will solve any problem anywhere, any time: Be filled with the Spirit." That became the theme of all my sharing for the next year or two.

Then I can remember sitting in a Greek class one day and having the truth of election dawn on me — the truth of God's elective purposes and how God chooses His people. I realized how special it was to be chosen of God, and I broke into tears as I saw that God had chosen me and bestowed His plenteous grace on me. It brought a revolutionary change in my life. It changed my way of thinking about everything.

Then I thought, "Everybody needs to know that." And I went around trying to explain election to everyone. The answer to everybody's problem was election, and I became an evangelist for that doctrine just as I had been an evangelist for "Jesus is Lord" and "being filled with the Spirit."

When the emphasis on spiritual warfare came along, I said: "That's it. That's been our problem all along. We've been fighting the devil, and we thought we were fighting each other. We've been caught up in a flesh and blood battle while the devil has been beating our brains out in the spiritual realm, and we didn't even know he was working. We've been ignoring the devil. We have to find out about warfare. If we ever learn that, we've got it." Warfare is important to know, but it's not the last word. If you don't learn it, you won't learn the next word. You can't jump from childhood to fatherhood without going through adolescence. You must be open to warfare and every aspect of it. God will teach you. Be strong in the Word, understanding your identity in Christ Jesus, your righteousness and your overcoming nature. But this is not the last word. It is only the young man's stage.

Others have had experiences different from mine that they allowed to become the last word. In the baptism of the Holy Spirit they have received a particular gift, such as tongues or healing, and have said: "That's it." And they have become evangelists for that experience. We can say of them, "They shouldn't do that;" but none of us should do it. It is a childlike behavior, an act of immaturity, to think your latest revelation is the epitome of all truth. Let's not stone one another for immaturity; instead let's love one another, realizing that we are all learning.

If you are unwilling to go to the Lord with a repentant heart, you are going to miss the next step because God is changing some things about you. Some things which you believe today, if you walk with Jesus, you won't be believing tomorrow, because He is taking away all the false concepts. He is restoring the truth.

Now what is the next stage of growth found in I John 2? As you move out of the young man's stage, you move into the fatherhood stage. God has a few of these around who have reached that stage. They have expanded their consciousness beyond the family, beyond victory and into a consciousness of eternity.

John said two different things to the children and to the young men. To the children, he said: "I write to you because your sins are forgiven, and I have written unto you because you know the Father." To the young men he said two things: "I have written to you because you have overcome the evil one," and "I have written to you because the Word of God abides in you." But to the Father he said the same thing twice. He said: "I am writing to you because you know Him who is from the beginning." In other words: "You have a consciousness of eternity. You are learning to see as God sees. You are learning to know as God knows. You are discovering your unity with the Father."

Jesus lived in this stage, obviously, because Jesus was constantly aware that He and the Father were one. He never had any sense of isolation or disagreement. Therefore, He was confident. He did not fret over decisions. When He got into a situation where He was to minister, He was so conscious that He and the Father were one, so sure that the Father would tell Him what to do anytime, that He knew no fear. He never fretted, as some of us do: "Oh, what will I do if I get out there and don't know what to do?" He knew the Father would tell Him because of the unity of their fellowship.

We say those familiar phrases, such as, "I am in Christ and Christ is in me, and we are one with the Father," but when we start practicing we say, "Oh, what if God doesn't show up?" We let fear and trepidation take over. In Matthew 10:16-20, where Jesus is telling the disciples how to live, He says:

'Behold, I send you out as sheep in the midst of wolves; therefore be shrewd as serpents, and innocent as doves. But beware of men; for they will deliver you up to the courts, and scourge you in their synagogues; and you shall even be brought before governors and kings for my sake, as a testimony to them and to the Gentiles. But when they deliver you up, do not become anxious about how or what you will speak; for it shall be given you in that hour what you are to speak. For it is not you who speak, but it is the Spirit of your Father who speaks in you.'

Do you know that you have the Spirit of the Father in you? If you are conscious that the Spirit of the Father is in you, that you and He are one, when you get into a situation demanding that you know what to say, who can you depend on? The Spirit of the Father. He will speak. What is it that has kept us from confidently witnessing all these years? The thought: "I'm afraid I won't know what to say." Why are we afraid to encounter a demon? "Well, how will I know which demon it is? How will I know what to tell it? What is the proper formula?" You don't need a formula if you're conscious of your unity with the Father. The instructions continue in verse 21:

'And brother will deliver up brother to death, and a father his child; and children will rise up against parents, and cause them to be put to death. And you will be hated by all on account of My name, but it is the one who has endured to the end who will be saved. But whenever they persecute you in this city, flee to the next; for truly I say to you, you shall not finish going through the cities of Israel, until the Son of Man comes. A disciple is not above his teacher, nor a slave above his master. It is enough for the disciple that he become as his teacher, and the slave as his master. If they have called the head of the house Beelzebub, how much more the members of his household.'

Look closely at verses 26 & 27: "'Therefore do not fear them, for there is nothing covered that will not be revealed, and hidden that will not be known. What I tell you in the darkness, speak in the light; and what you hear whispered in your ear, proclaim upon the housetops.'" That may have many applications, but let me emphasize one that is most important. He is saying: "Listen, do not fear the unknown. When you get into a difficult situation, anything you need to know, in that moment, I will reveal to you." We are afraid we won't know the unknown. We think: "I'm going to get out on a limb and God is going to cut it off behind me." But He said: "Anything you need to know when you get involved in ministry, I will reveal to you. And then what I tell you, I want you to speak it."

You may think, "Oh, no; if I tell them what God is saying to me, they are going to say I'm crazy." But the Lord says, beginning in verse 28:

> 'And do not fear those who kill the body, but are unable to kill the soul; but rather fear Him who is able to destroy both souls and body in hell. Are not two sparrows sold for a cent? And yet not one of them will fall to the ground apart from your Father. But all the very hairs of your head are all numbered. Therefore do not fear; you are of more value than many sparrows.'

Jesus is trying to instill in His disciples a consciousness of eternity, the consciousness that you are one with the Father, that the Father is committed to you. Everything He has He has committed to you, as long as you are committed to His purposes.

One of the ways you know when you have an eternity consciousness is that your focus is totally on others. When you are in the childhood stage, your focus is largely on yourself. "My sins are forgiven." "My Father loves me." "I can go crawl up in the arms of my Father." "I can talk to my Father." "My Father listens to me." "My Father loves me." "My Father knows when I'm sick and He knows when I hurt." "My Father will teach me." Where is the consciousness? It is on yourself, on you and what God has done or can do for you. That is not bad because it is not a selfishness, but a consciousness of your child-Father relationship with God.

As you grow into the young man's stage, consciousness then is on your victory, on what God has given to you. Consciousness has moved from just you to what you have. "I have armor." "I have victory." "I have warfare." "I have authority." "I have power." It is my arsenal that has become my focus.

But when you move on to the mature fatherhood stage, you begin to think as God thinks. The thoughts that begin to prevail are along the line of: "For God so loved the world..." Where is his focus? On others. Always others. He is seeing the need. He is loving. He is giving. It is not, "What truth can I learn to get victory?" It is, "What truth can I learn to enable me to minister life?" It is not, "Somebody come pray over me so I can have power to be somebody." It is, "I'm willing to receive power so I can minister life." The important thing, though, is to be a channel, never the reservoir. We become channels for others. Freely I have received, freely I want to give.

That is where we are going — to the fatherhood stage. Don't despair at the childhood stage or the young man's stage. But we are going on to the stage which our focus is on others, and we are conscious of our unity with the Father. In that stage, we are aware that all He has is ours. It is available to us. We can have it but only to use. We don't have to sit on it. We discover its effectiveness only when we get into ministry situations and need it.

We see in Psalm 91 a consciousness that frees the believer to be useful. This is a consciousness you can have and you must constantly have, especially during the fatherhood stage. Otherwise, you can't be free to keep others in your focus. The Psalm says:

> He who dwells in the shelter of the Most High will abide in the shadow of the Almighty."

That gives the impression of a close relationship, doesn't it? If you are in someone's shadow, you are very close.

> I will say to the Lord, 'My refuge and my fortress, my God, in whom I trust!' For it is He who delivers you from the snare of the trapper, and from the deadly pestilence. He will cover you with His pinions, and under His wings you may seek refuge; His faithfulness is a shield and bulwark.

That is what you learn in the young man's stage. In the baby stage, you think your faithfulness is the issue. "I have to be faithful. It is how much I can believe." You find out that the issue is not how much you can believe; it is how much He is committed to you. The issue is His faithfulness. His faithfulness produces your faith. Continuing with verse 5:

> You will not be afraid of the terror by night, or of the arrow that flies by day; of the pestilence that stalks in darkness, or of the destruction that lays waste at noon.

You see, the enemy attacks at night, day, darkness and noon. If you are in the shade of the Almighty, the time of day is of no consequence. Verse 7 continues:

> A thousand may fall at your side, and ten thousand at your right hand; but it shall not approach you. You will only look on with your eyes and see the recompense of the wicked.

Have you ever noticed how fear tends to well up in you when you see people falling all around you? The devil likes to say: "You think you are doing so well! I want to show you some people who thought that. Remember that fellow who was really spiritual and walked with God? Well, look what has happened to him." If your consciousness is on victory or even on yourself, you will be in serious trouble. You had better be conscious of your union with the Father. When you are, it doesn't matter if others fall all around you. That is not your focus anyway. You will only look on with your eyes and see the recompense of the wicked. The Psalmist continues:

> For you have made the Lord, my refuge, even the Most High, your dwelling place. No evil will befall you. Nor will any plague come near your tent. For He will give His angels charge concerning you, to guard you in all your ways. They will bear you up in their hands, lest you strike your foot against a stone. You will tread upon the lion and cobra, the young lion and the serpent you will trample down.

In this Psalm you are seeing the consciousness of a man who was absolutely convinced that the Father was committed to him. In the fatherhood stage, you live with this consciousness of unity and eternity. You see things from the end to the beginning. In union with God, you know as God knows.

How does God know? A dear brother asked me this question one time. He said, "How does God know? Does God have to think in order to know?" No, God doesn't have to think to know. He doesn't have to deduce or to induce. He just knows. And when you move into eternity consciousness there are things you just know. You know spiritually and you know eternally.

Have you ever prayed at one time or another, "Lord, I want to be like Jesus?" I hope you have. Normally when we talk about wanting to be like Jesus, what we mean is that we would like to behave as Jesus did. We would like to be able to forgive as He forgave, to love as He loved and minister as He ministered. But to behave as Jesus did, we must know as Jesus knows. If we are asking God to make us like Jesus, we will have to understand the place He begins to do this. He doesn't start with the behavior.

Jesus starts with the knowing. What is it that He knows? "I and the Father are One." "The Father has committed judgment to Me." He knew that the resources of the Father were at His disposal. He didn't wait until He could see or feel them. He knew it. And, knowing it, He used them, and the Father worked with Him.

That is the first step in being like Jesus — knowing as Jesus knows; becoming conscious of unity with the Father and our usefulness in His hands. With that consciousness, we can be the Church.

Do you know where you are in this growth scale? Don't despise the stage of growth you are in. Be patient and lay a solid foundation for the next stage of your spiritual growth.

If you are in the childhood stage, know what God is saying to you and enjoy Him at that level. He is trying to teach you two things: the freedom of forgiveness and what it means to relate to God as Father. If you don't have those things down and you move into the young man's stage and try to learn warfare, you will be constantly beaten down. Learn what you are supposed to know as a child.

If you are in a young man's stage, God is trying to teach you that you are an overcomer. Learn who you are in Christ. He is trying to teach you to be strong in the Word. There will be nothing more important for you at this stage than to get in the Word and let God teach it to you.

But don't stop anywhere until you have moved into that eternal knowing, until the heart of God is throbbing in you, until what God cares about is what you care about.

What does God care about? He cares for people. He loved them so much that He sent His Son into the world. That's the kind of heart you have when you are conscious of your unity with the Father. Houses and land, money and things mean absolutely nothing except as tools. People ministering to people, bringing the life of Jesus to people — that is the heart of God. Until that is in your heart, you have not arrived where He wants you to be.

Don't live in condemnation. Don't sit around saying, "Oh, I'm not there. What am I going to do ?" Find out where you are and start growing at that level. If God is moving you into another stage, go on and do the things of that stage, but never try to measure your own maturity by where others are. A one-year-old still needs diapers but he may be a perfectly mature one-year-old. Now if he becomes fifteen and still needs diapers then there is a problem, but at one he is just fine.

You may have been fretting because of burdens in your heart for people, but you didn't know what to do. You thought, "Well, I guess I need to call the pastor." Quit calling others; do it yourself. You may say, "I'm just not sure I can." You can't! *He can.* And that is where you need to move — to the stage at which you know your union with Him and know He will do it.

Do you honestly believe you are in the childhood stage? Do you wonder if you have ever been born again? You can't be a child until you are born. That is not meant to insult you. I just want you to be honest because I can tell you how to be born and get into childhood in the Father's family. You can be born again and know that your sins are forgiven for His sake. You can quit wondering who God is, and you can know Him as a Father, be held next to His bosom, and be taught by Him. If you are not in the family, I invite you to come to the family by receiving Jesus as your Savior by faith.

Do you believe you have moved into the young man's stage? Here there is warfare, but there are also victories. Are you in the fatherhood stage?

It can be very helpful for us to understand what stage we're in, but we must not be so segmentation conscious that we say, "I'm not doing anything else until I find out which stage I am in." You may be somewhere in between stages. Fretting over it can put you in bondage and make you stagnant.

My purpose has been simply to help you understand what God is teaching you, where He is taking you and what is going to happen to you. The idea is not to look for a stage at which you can settle down. You are to venture on out. If you are in childhood or young man's stage, you can miss a lot by saying: "I'm going to wait until I'm at the fatherhood stage." The disciples did some exciting things as babes. They went out and came back saying: "Lord, the demons are subject to us." That's not too bad for babes! And they were doing that before the Holy Spirit came in the way we know Him. So don't be saying, "Well, I'm just a baby, and I'm going to stay in my crib for the next ten years before I move into fatherhood." Go on *now*. You've got all the necessary equipment. Start being the Church.

Chapter Ten

What Is Church-Life?

A pastor of a large denominational church had announced on Sunday evening that there would be a meeting of the board in his office after the service. When he arrived he found several people from the congregation that he did not even recognize. When he said to them, "I don't believe that I remember you being a part of the board," the response was, "If you can get anymore 'bored' than we are, we would like to see it!"

The Problem of "Church-Life"

The problem with the phrase "Church-Life" is that it normally carries with it connotations of boredom. The phrase itself is not a marketable phrase. Very few people will pick up a book entitled "Church-Life." When the pastor announces that he is going to preach on "Church-Life" nobody gets too excited. We have identified "Church-Life" with the crystallization of our culture, comforts and traditions of the past. It seems that we have been doomed to take an alive work of God, categorize it, analyze it and reduce it to a lifeless form. Therefore, for most of us, "Church-Life" consists of many meetings but very few times of excitement and stimulation.

In the past, it seems that as soon as a work of God was recognized as such, men and women began to analyze it, categorize it and declare what was "of God," and what was "in excess" and wound up reducing "Church-Life" to some kind of predictable form. We have many denominations that have come from the moving of the fresh wind of the Spirit at different times in our history. When the move is over, however, "Church-Life" seems to be reduced to people who meet but don't relate, sing but don't praise and preach but don't prophesy.

Meeting vs. Relating

A zealous Baptist brother was speaking to a friend who was a member of another denominational church. This brother incredulously asked him, "Why aren't you a Baptist?" The man responded, "I am not physically able." We sometimes ascribe the aggressiveness in meetings only to Baptists. But it seems that every church turns their "Church-Life" into meetings, and they all happen down at the church house. Evidence of New Testament "Church-Life" is not so much "meeting" but "relating." It seems that many times we come to a meeting and, even if we have no clear direction from God about the decisions to be made, we feel that a decision *must* be made because we had a meeting. I'm finding that it is much better to relate to one another and, when a clear decision comes, it will be recognized by those who are responsible to make the decision and implement it.

Recently, I had a wonderful experience with the elders at our church. We spent two days together walking, hunting with our bird dogs, and having fellowship with each other. The difference in this approach and a formal meeting is that when you sit around the meeting table with an agenda over a specific issue, it seems the pressure is on to talk even when you have nothing to say and to decide even when the decision is not clear. The true purpose for meeting is to relate to one another's hearts and bless one another. That way, the conversation comes naturally, and decisions that need to be made will be surfaced by the Spirit of God who dwells in us. It was a refreshing experience to walk through the fields with no pressure to say anything unless there was something to say. We found ourselves walking sometimes for an hour or more without saying a word, and then drifting together as we walked and discussed issues that surfaced in our hearts. And now they had life and we were not only able to bless one another, but to hear the voice of God.

Singing vs. Praising

The next problem with our concept of "Church-Life" is that we sing but we don't praise. Music has always had a vital part in "Church-Life." When God moves, there is not only beauty and life in what He does but there is harmony. It is something that God has built into His life. When we take the music that was a result of the life of God and reduce it to a form, we simply become "singers" of the songs rather than "praisers" of the God who gave the songs.

Preaching vs. Prophesying

The next problem is that we preach but we don't prophesy. Many pastors wonder why they preach but see no results of life in their churches. Many are confused because they "preach the Bible" every Sunday but their numbers are dwindling and there is no supernatural, exciting life happening. The simple definition of prophesying would help us understand the difference in preaching and prophesying. Prophecy is "a Spirit-filled proclamation of who Christ is and what that means to this situation." Prophecy can be a personal word to an individual, a corporate word to a congregation or a national or international word to even larger groups of people. But, if it is true prophecy, it will center around who Christ is and what that means to the current situation.

The Essence of Christ

Meeting without relating, singing without praising, preaching without prophesying — it is not right for us to accept this preconceived understood form as "Church-Life." "Church-Life" in essence is the very life of Jesus expressed through His body on the earth. **"Church-Life" today is to be no less exciting nor less supernatural than the life that Jesus expressed through His physical body when He was here on the earth.** It was His "life" that He gave to us. It was His "life" that the Holy Spirit breathed into the Church on the day of Pentecost. It is His "life" that we can expect to experience and express as we live on the earth. Why then do we settle for such poor substitutes of the life of Christ? If life is a gift, why have we not received it and used it?

Maybe part of the answer can come from our understanding of the fall of man. God had put within man the ability to organize, categorize, and rule. When man fell, that ability was perverted and it seems that man inevitably takes what is life and reduces it to organized, categorized, analyzed death. When Jesus was on the earth, He was the *very* Word of God and life of God expressed through a physical body. His greatest problem, however, was with those who had taken the word of God from the past, analyzed it, organized it, categorized it, and refused to let life in. What they had was understandable, comfortable, traditional and controllable. Jesus, on the other hand, was exciting, supernatural, and out of their control.

An interesting period of time in Jesus' life is recorded in Matthew chapter 9 starting with verse 18 where it says that a synagogue official had a daughter who was sick and ultimately died. He came to Jesus and asked for help. On His way to help, Jesus ran into a woman who had an issue of blood and He ministered to her. Then immediately upon leaving her, He healed some blind men and then healed a man who was dumb because of demons. At the end of the chapter the Scripture says that Jesus had compassion on all these multitudes because they were like sheep having no shepherd. The interesting thing is that they had many church officials but no shepherds. When Jesus said, "Pray the Lord of the harvest that He would send out workers," He was asking for shepherds.

The Role of the Shepherd

One of the reasons that we have so much death and destruction among the people of God today is that we have been content to have church officials but not shepherds. We have reduced the role of a shepherd to a "C.E.O." or an administrator or ruler. We have forced pastors into roles that they neither want nor are able to perform, so burnout is a constant companion to many who are in "full-time Christian vocation." What God is about during these days is raising up people who have a shepherd's heart.

A shepherd is not necessarily a ruler. Shepherds are people who care for sheep. The wonderful thing about being a shepherd in God's Kingdom is that we are shepherds under the Great Shepherd. It is not our ultimate responsibility to guide the sheep, feed the sheep, or protect the sheep. It is our responsibility under the Great Shepherd to facilitate all of these things. Jesus said that His sheep hear His voice. That means that *all* of the sheep can hear the Great Shepherd's voice — which releases the shepherds from the pressure of having to make ultimate decisions of truth and error. Jesus is a faithful Shepherd; therefore, He is going to protect His sheep. I simply need to be obedient to Him and say what He says and do what He does. As I recognize Him as the Great Shepherd, being an under-shepherd becomes a wonderful challenge and blessing. God is calling for thousands of ordinary folks to be shepherds, whose goal in life will be to turn other sheep into shepherds themselves. The quality of our "Church-Life" will dramatically improve when we have fewer church officials and more shepherds.

The Role of the Church

One of the tendencies we have when we look at the poor state of "Church-Life" is to become critical and condemning. Obviously, it never does any good to curse the darkness. Rather, we should discover the life and the light. But it is *not* wrong to ask questions when things are not working well. A Westinghouse executive, when asked how to determine the success of an organization, simply said, "When we want to know if we are successful we ask only two questions. What is our product and are we producing it?" Though the church is technically an organism, and not an organization, that is still not a bad question for any of us to ask. What is the product of the Church, and are we producing it? Since God's Church is an agency of redemption, then the product of the Church would be to produce fully redeemed people. It really wouldn't hurt if the church reestablished that purpose periodically — to produce a fully redeemed people, people who realize that they were brought out of depravity themselves because God saw value in them. And now because they have been brought out they have the capacity to redeem others.

Remember the Kingdom parable that Jesus told about the man who found a treasure hidden in a field? It was of such great value that he went and did whatever was necessary to buy the field in order to get the treasure. That is exactly what God did for us. He saw fallen man in the field, which is the world, and saw such great value in him — even though he was dead, perverted and bound in his sins — that He sent His only Son to pay the price necessary to buy man out of that pitiful plight. He brought man out, made him His child, and released him to be all that he could be. You are God's treasure — even though it may be difficult to believe.

When we are redeemed we are able to look at everything that the Devil has perverted in this world and see the intrinsic value that God placed there. For too long the church has given up on things that the Devil has perverted and relegated them to "this old world." I am tired of us giving things to Satan that don't belong to him. It is not right for him to have the arts, the music, the dance, the theater, drama, the media, the press, etc. Everything created on this earth was created by God and was stamped good by Him. The Devil has perverted it, but those with a redemptive perspective can see the intrinsic value and can buy back those things by the authority and power that has been given them through Jesus' name. We have the capacity to look into the face of the drug addict, the homosexual, the broken, the depressed, and the mental patient and to redeem that which has been previously destroyed.

One of the things that will help us is understanding that redemption is a process. Since the church is an organism rather than an organization, then it has life. Things that have life grow in several different ways. They grow internally in interdependence as each part does its own work. They grow quantitatively as they get bigger, and they grow in maturity as they learn how to fit into the grand scheme of things.

The Call of God

Another of the misconceptions that has thwarted "Church-Life" in the past has been the misunderstanding of the call of God. God's call to men is a call to believe — not just in a new set of facts, but in a *Person*. For too long we have defined evangelism in terms of believing some facts. We have considered a person converted when they quit believing some bad facts and started believing some new facts. In reality, these facts are presented only to get the person to believe in Jesus Christ. If there is no personal relationship with Jesus Christ, there is no redemption or conversion. Too many people have been "saved" by making a decision to believe three or four facts that were presented to them, and yet they never made the next step of faith to relate to the individual, Jesus Christ. The church field is scattered with doubting, fearful people who are not really sure that if they died they would go to heaven. They are not sure that they were sincere enough when they made their decision. They feel guilty and condemned because they have sinned since their decision and have basically been taught that saved people don't commit gross sins. This confusion could be cleared up if they could understand that salvation is a call to relate to God through Jesus Christ.

The Body of Christ

But the call of God is even something beyond that. It is a call to belong to His body. It becomes complicated if we declare that people can be saved and healthy in isolation and alienation from the body of Christ. This is simply not true.

The call of God is for us to belong to His body — to be an integral part of the church, if you will. A person is never going to experience the actual life of Christ expressed until he is an interdependent, interrelating member of the body. The truth is, all of us have a natural inclination to want to belong to something. We saw it in our youth when the boys developed their little clubs and had to have a password to get in; when the girls all got together and had their little secret cliques. This does not diminish as we get older. When we go to college we divide up into sororities and fraternities. Then we pick our church denominations and our country clubs, etc. It is amazing what people will go through just to be a part of something.

I distinctly remember when I was a freshman in college that I had the opportunity to be initiated into the athletic club in our school. I "lettered" my freshman year in football and then came the big day to be received into the athlete's club. On that great day the upper classmen made me chew dog biscuits during the day. They would offer for the quenching of my thirst a concoction they had made from combining their tobacco juice with alum water. You say, "Oh, how gross!" Exactly! Yet I was willing to endure that to be a part of the group. But it did not end there. Later that day they took all of us who were being initiated fifteen miles from town, stripped us of our clothes, poured syrup over our body and covered us with corn flakes. They sprayed paint on our heads and told us that if we could get back to town we would be received into the club. I thought this was wonderful and gladly did what was necessary to be a part.

The fact is that everybody wants to be received and accepted. Too much of the time we have used church membership to let people have a shallow sense of belonging. The call of God is to *really* belong, to be a part of, to be a giving, receiving, integral part of His body.

Measuring Growth

If we ask direct, specific questions about three areas of measurable growth, we can get an idea about the health of our "Church-Life." These areas are: growth of mutual ministry, quantity, and maturity. First, let's look at the eternal growth of mutual ministry.

Mutual Ministry

God has given gifts to everyone in the Body of Christ. To the degree that we recognize our gifts and release them in supporting and enabling the organism to grow, we ourselves are growing in this area. The question we could ask an individual believer is "Do you know what your spiritual gift or gifts are and are you in the process of learning how to use them?" The church that has been convinced that there are no spiritual gifts or that they are not very important would lack a great deal of the very life of Christ. No wonder the enemy has spent so much time convincing us that gifts have been abused and therefore they must be rejected. That is simply not the case. The church who refuses to receive the gifts of God and to use them in a healthy, wholesome way will be a church that does not experience the true life of God. If you do not know your spiritual gifts make it a goal in your life to know they are by this time next year and to be a part of some group of Christians who are learning to use the gifts properly.

The Quantity of Growth

The second area is the area of quantity in redeeming the world around you. The question could be asked, "Do you relate to anyone who has the need to be redeemed by Jesus Christ and to belong to His body?" We're not pushing here the old mentality of feeling guilty because there are lost people in the world. Instead, we need the perspective that because I have a life that is worth enjoying and experiencing I can share it with others. I encourage you to get rid of the mentality of "I'm going to *win* my community" and adopt the mentality of "I'm going to *love* my community." As you relate to others they will see the life of God in you. If they see the life of God you will not have to "win" them to a theological or intellectual argument — they will ask you about the hope that lies within you. In that relationship you can share Jesus with many. We have given most of the credit for those who have been converted to the few who have the gift of evangelism. We watch someone stand on a stage, give an altar call and have thousands respond — and we say "that person won them all to Jesus." The truth is that there was much influence throughout the years through individuals who won't be recognized until we get to heaven: the mother who prayed, the friends who shared, the encouraging words that came from strangers, the printed piece that happened to be lying on the desk. So many of these influences led to the ultimate conversion. The evangelist was simply the one who drew the net.

Growth in Maturity

The next area of growth is the area of maturity. Every organism that is healthy grows in its interrelationships of its own parts, grows physically, and grows in maturity. With maturity it learns to relate to the world in which it lives. Maturity could be measured spiritually in terms of one word: stewardship. To what degree have you become a steward, rather than owner over everything that God has entrusted to you? The person who has not had his money, his time, his priorities, and his talents under the proper stewardship is one who is not growing in maturity. Jesus has said if you are not trustworthy with little, you will not be given much. In that context He was speaking of money or possessions. These questions could help you in evaluating your growth and maturity: 1) Are you the steward or the owner of your money? 2) Are you honest about your weaknesses? 3) Do you voluntarily submit to someone for accountability?

What a privilege it is to live in this world and have divine life in our bosoms. What a privilege it is to have been given the resurrected life of Jesus expressed in this world. What a shame it is that we have reduced that life to some kind of form or ritual. What a shame that when the world thinks about "Church-Life" they think about steeples, stained glass, programs and boredom. We can be a part of generation that changes that. We can be willing to be the body of Christ that expresses the life of God to the world.

THE EMMAUS ROAD
Ministry School

EMMAUS ROAD **Ministry School** is a nine month period of intensive training in the practical aspects of Christian life. Many subjects are taught at Emmaus Road that colleges and seminaries leave out, such as deliverance, spiritual warfare, praying for the sick, inner healing, and more. Emmaus Road does not try to replace a broad based education for receiving a traditional degree, but specializes in practical areas of equipping for ministry in the shortest possible time.

Also, some of the instructors at EMMAUS ROAD **Ministry School** are considered among the top teachers and Christian leaders in the nation, including Millard Box, Don Crossland, John Deal, Jack Deere, Rick Godwin, Dan Hall, Dudley Hall, Jim Hylton, Peter Lord, Ralph Neighbor, Jeanne Rogers, John & Beverley Sheasby, Jim Tuell, Doug White, and Clark Whitten. Guest teachers include, Mike Bickle, Paul Cain, Francis Frangipane, Rick Joyner, James Robison and others. These all work together to give a broad and challenging perspective of ministry and service to the Lord.

The school is open to all ages, male and female — those called to full-time ministry and those who want to be more effective in their own local church. Every church member would profit and be blessed from attending the school, but particularly pastors, praise leaders, home group leaders, youth pastors and ministry teams.

For more information, please call or write to:

EMMAUS ROAD MINISTRY SCHOOL
P.O. Box 400213
Euless, TX 76040
(817) 545-0282

About the Publisher

MorningStar Publications is a non-profit organization dedicated to promulgating important teachings and timely prophetic messages to the whole body of Christ. We also desire to promote interchange between the different streams within the body. Other parts of the vision of MorningStar include the establishing of a Ministry Center, Teaching Center, House of Prophets, Intercessory Prayer and Worship Center, Sabbath Rest Center and Publishing Center.

For additional information or for a free catalog of books, tapes, and other materials published by MorningStar, write to:

MorningStar Publications
P.O. Box 369
Pineville, NC 28134

MorningStar
PUBLICATIONS